the edible landscape

CREATING A BEAUTIFUL AND BOUNTIFUL GARDEN
WITH VEGETABLES, FRUITS AND FLOWERS

EMILY TEPE

Photography by Paul Markert

Voyageur Press

Special thanks to the organizations and individuals who graciously allowed us to photograph their gardens and landscapes: Como Park Zoo and Conservatory, Jane and Jim Gilbert, Maureen Hark, Charlene McEvoy and Doug Olson, Laura McGuire, Minnesota Landscape Arboretum, Theresa Rooney, Dawn Spraungel, and Julie Weisenhorn.

First published in 2012 by Voyageur Press, an imprint of MBI Publishing Company, 400 First Avenue North, Suite 300, Minneapolis, MN, 55401 USA

MBI Publishing Company titles are also available at discounts in bulk quantity for industrial or sales-promotional use. For details write to Special Sales Manager at MBI Publishing Company, 400 First Avenue North, Suite 300, Minneapolis, MN, 55401 USA

ISBN: 978-0-7603-4139-1

Library of Congress Cataloging-in-Publication Data

Tepe, Emily.
  The edible landscape : creating a beautiful and bountiful garden with vegetables, fruits and flowers / by Emily Tepe.
     p. cm.
  Includes index.
  ISBN 978-0-7603-4139-1
  1. Edible landscaping. 2. Landscape gardening. I. Title.
  SB475.9.E35T47 2013
  635.9--dc23
                          2012022654

Acquisitions editor: Kari Cornell
Editor: Melinda Keefe
Design manager: Cindy Samargia Laun
Designer: Sandra Salamony
Layout: Erin Fahringer

Back cover illustration: Chandler O'Leary (anagram-press.com)

Printed in China

contents

preface

FOOD, GARDENS, AND A CREATIVE SPIRIT

I'll tell you right now, I am not a landscape designer. In fact, I'm not even a lifelong, well-seasoned gardener. For those of you who have not put the book back on the shelf after reading those two sentences, thank you for giving me a chance to explain. I am simply a person who loves to eat fresh food and spend time outdoors growing that food. I appreciate the unique forms, textures, and colors of food plants, and I enjoy the challenge of making those plants look as delicious as they taste. I believe that anyone can and should grow some of their own food and that doing so doesn't have to mean setting aside part of the yard to be the "vegetable garden." It simply means taking a look at tomatoes, cabbage, blueberries,

A sturdy arbor elevates these cold-hardy grapes, creating a striking entrance to this garden. The structure exposes the plants to the sunlight, allowing the fruit to dangle within easy reach.

The fruit of the bell pepper plant is not only a crisp addition to salads and stir-fries but also makes a statement in the garden with its shiny, deeply colored, oblong form. The immense range of pepper varieties ensures there's something for everyone, both in terms of color in the garden and flavor on the plate.

and lettuce a little differently and giving them a place in the landscape just as you would clematis, hostas, azaleas, and impatiens. With a little creativity, and a desire to have fresh food right outside your door, I believe a yard can be both beautiful and productive.

HEAVY ON INSPIRATION

This book isn't intended to be a how-to on every issue of planning and maintaining a garden. Rather, I hope to inspire you to grow some of your own food, right in your landscape. We will touch on a lot of factors that are important in any kind of garden: soil, light, plant nutrition, insect pests, diseases; and you'll get some suggestions, opinions, and stories about things that have worked for me. What I'd like to do is inspire you take note of these details and give them some thought. I hope to introduce you to or remind you why they're important considerations for a successful garden. However, for the most part I hope to spark your imagination and get you thinking of the many exciting and attractive ways you might incorporate food plants into your landscape.

IS IT A FRUIT OR A VEGETABLE?

Throughout this book, I sometimes refer to peppers, tomatoes, eggplants, and such as "fruits." When I call them that I am referring to the parts that we eat . . . the actual pepper, tomato, or eggplant. I call them fruits because that is biologically what they are. Elsewhere, however, I refer to the plants as vegetables, and that is because of our cultural understanding of vegetables and fruits. In discussing various plants, and in the appendix at the back of this book, I categorize plants as vegetables, fruits, herbs, or flowers. Plants we traditionally consider vegetables are categorized as vegetables, even though the actual part we eat I call a fruit. Make sense?

NORTHERN GARDENS AND BEYOND

Having lived much of my life in the Upper Midwest, I am most accustomed to the growing conditions in this region. As I've learned and practiced gardening, and sought advice and inspiration, I've often found gardening books tend to be written by those in warmer climates. While their words and photos are inspiring, they're sometimes unrealistic for someone contending with as few as 120 frost-free days and winters that see plenty of nights in the negative 20s. Consequently, this book tends to focus on plants that can be grown in cooler regions. However, the principles, ideas, and inspiration in the book certainly apply to most gardens in any region, and you'll see in the Appendix that I've included some plant options that are better-suited to warmer regions.

EMILY'S 10 FAVORITES LISTS

As you page through the book, you'll come across a number of "Emily's 10 Favorites" lists. Plants make it into these lists because they meet two very important criteria: the plant has merit in the category of the list, for example attracting beneficial insects or growing well in the shade, but it also has great aesthetic appeal and value in the landscape. Now, if you're ready to give those fruits and veggies a whole new life in your yard, read on!

Northern gardeners contend with challenges such as early snowfall and late-spring frosts. Garden thyme is a hardy perennial in most regions and generally withstands early-season snow and cold temperatures, maintaining its green color throughout. AUTHOR PHOTO

Bay leaves provide a lovely deep flavor when added to sauces, soups, and stews. These flavorful leaves grow on attractive trees that look stately in the garden, especially when surrounded by lower-growing herbs such as thyme and dill.

introduction
the garden is returning home

This country is experiencing a revolution. It's in the news, it's in best-selling books, it's on blogs, TV, and film. I'm not talking about politics or protest, I'm talking about food: food that's fresh, pure, local, and delicious. We have had our fill of tasteless, woody tomatoes from the far reaches of the globe. We have decided once and for all that a peach should be juicy and sweet, not pithy and tart. We have begun to understand the true cost of food traveling to our tables from distant corners of the planet. We are tasting again, thanks to farmers markets and local co-ops, the real flavors we remember from our childhoods or have heard about in stories from our parents and grandparents. These are the flavors of freshly

Food plants can be just as attractive as ornamental plants in the garden. The slender, straight leaves and soft, blue-green color of garlic contrast nicely with the broad fleshy leaves of chard (background) and the bright colors of the zinnias in the foreground.

These freshly harvested vegetables look as delicious as they taste. The bright, bold colors of tomatoes, cucumbers, radishes, and purple basil fill the garden with a kaleidoscope of color before they are picked to brighten the salad bowl.

picked fruits and vegetables brimming with deliciousness, tasting like the sun, carried lovingly to the table in the gathered corners of an apron or in a weathered wicker basket. Carried a few feet, not thousands of miles.

All this talk and all these changes are inspiring millions of people to start growing their own food. People are growing food in places we never would have imagined: rooftops, abandoned parking lots, balconies overlooking huge cities, and tiny backyards on the average city street. Individuals and families are taking up the trowel and discovering that growing food can be fun, fulfilling, and, ultimately, delicious. They are taking control of what they eat, where it comes from, and what goes into it and on it. Families are reclaiming their food and finding it is very, very good.

Yes, politics and protest are definitely parts of the story, but I'll leave that discussion to others for now. What I want to talk about here is a bit less fiery. I want to talk about plants. Food plants in particular, but not exclusively. And along with plants I want to talk about yards: front, back, side, and every little corner. I want to talk about putting all this together—food plants, ornamental plants, and yards—with creativity and inspiration. I want to talk about the joy of growing one's own food in beautiful, thoughtful gardens overflowing with color and flavor. I want to talk about the delight of trial and error, the wisdom that can result, and the amazing things that can be discovered from the simple act of growing a few plants. I want to talk about the fulfillment of planning a garden and seeing the result. And through all this, I hope you will be inspired to look at your own yard and imagine the possibilities. You see, no longer does "vegetable garden" have to mean a rectangle relegated to the back corner of the yard with long, straight rows of cabbage or tomatoes. As this country gets more crowded and more of us live in urban areas with small yards, or no yards at all to speak of, we need to become a bit more creative with how we grow our own food.

Creating an attractive and productive garden in a small space might seem impossible, especially if you're faced with urban features like compacted soil, chain-link fences or an old concrete patio. But if you let these limitations become inspiration, and use them to help guide your creativity, you'll be amazed at what you can dream up. Throughout this book you'll see examples of some wonderful things that can be done with a limited amount of space. From interesting plant combinations to unique structures and planting beds, you're bound to get some ideas that will work for you. Whether you have a small or large yard to work with, you'll find plenty of inspiring examples and good ideas to help incorporate food plants into your yard here and there or to completely recreate your yard as a masterpiece of color and flavor.

Just because you have a tiny space doesn't mean you can't grow food creatively. A few planters hanging on the wall of this tiny balcony burst with tomatoes and herbs. If space is limited, keep an eye out for interesting containers and try clever, space-saving ways like this to grow your plants.

A FRESH PERSPECTIVE

We generally reserve the concept of "ornamental" for plants with showy flowers. And while I don't intend to downplay the beauty or the value of those plants, I want to encourage you to stop and take a fresh look at the humble food plants and see them in an ornamental light. See them for what they can add to the visual quality of your landscape as well as for the food they provide. That's what this book is all about. It is time to free our fruits and veggies from the confines of the garden row and appreciate them for their looks as well as their flavor.

So now that you have banished from your mind the concept that vegetables and fruits must be grown in rows, and you're open to the idea that a tomato plant can be a striking addition to your landscape, let's explore some ideas for transforming your yard into a feast for the eyes and the table.

how to approach
your edible
landscape

MIXING IT UP

Before I dive into all the wonderful and exciting aspects of
landscaping with food plants, I want to square away a few things.
When you think of an "edible landscape" you may think of a
landscape that is entirely edible: where you could stroll through
and eat anything you see. As wonderful as that would be, not only
is it virtually impossible, it's not very practical. First, parts of many
food-producing plants are not edible at all (take rhubarb leaves, for
example), so the idea of planting a landscape where you could eat
anything you see would be extremely limiting. Second, if you

A simple greenhouse allows a gardener to get a jump on the season,
especially in northern climates, without filling up windowsills all over
the house. Given a little planning, such a structure can fit right into the
landscape, providing visual contrast among the plants.

planted only food plants, your landscape could end up consisting of almost entirely annuals (especially if you live in a cooler climate), which doesn't do much for year-round visual interest or soil building. Third, ornamental plants (perennials, annuals, shrubs, and trees) offer a lot of color and variety, attract beneficial insects, and help to diversify (which, by the way, does a great job at keeping pests and disease at bay). Sure, you could plant an entire landscape of food plants, but you would be missing a lot by doing that. That's why, in this book, we'll be talking about mixing all kinds of different plants: fruits, vegetables, herbs, annuals, perennials, shrubs, and trees to make the very best of the space you have, both visually and edibly.

This front yard garden captures the attention of anyone passing by. Only when visitors pause a moment do they realize that just about everything in the garden is edible. Ornamental zinnias provide a spark of color, but beyond those, chard, garlic, cucumbers, tomatoes, and squash make an attractive scene along this quiet city street.

In any garden, there's a special fulfillment that comes from digging in the soil, tending plants, and harvesting fresh food that you helped to grow. When surrounded by a beautiful array of plants, the chores in the garden become even more enjoyable. These leeks are backed by colorful chard.

CONNECTING WITH OUR FOOD

Why do we garden? With easy access to so much food these days, especially with farmers' markets popping up in many cities and towns, why do we bother gardening? I think one of the biggest reasons, whether we realize it or not, is connection. With the availability of so much food at any time of year, it can be difficult to see the connection between our food and the earth. Food is, without a doubt, one of the most important parts of our lives. And yet we let strangers, thousands of miles away, on land we will never s ee, decide what our food must look like and taste like, what our food is treated with to prevent disease, and what is put into the soil to make that food grow. We blindly accept strawberries that have little flavor, no color except for the thin veneer of red, simply because they are available and they are cheap. Why do we accept this? Why do we give these strangers such power? We do it because we have lost the sense of connection to one of the most critical, vital aspects of our lives—our food.

Those of us who sense this disconnection, in one form or another, find ourselves wanting to grow our own food. When we get into the garden and begin to understand soil, water, nutrients, and light, we see how connected it all is. When we tend the earth and nurture the plants it sustains, which will eventually sustain us, there is a sense of wholeness: something so innately fulfilling about connecting with the earth, with the source of our food.

a word about organic

Many of the techniques covered in this book will naturally help to reduce pests and diseases among your plants, and this is a very good thing. I'm one of those people who believe that potentially harmful chemicals have no place near my food or in my yard. This is not a treatise on organic gardening, nor is this an organic gardening guidebook. I may mention a couple of pest control methods I've tried, but the truth is I haven't tried many. That's because in my garden, I tend to let things happen as they will and don't go to great reactionary lengths to rid the garden of pests. If squash bugs infest my zucchini, I'm more likely to pull the plant out than to smash millions of bugs (ick) and spray the plants and all that. (However, if I notice the first batch of eggs on a leaf, I'll definitely give them a squish to try to save my plant.) My rationale is that I'm not focused on major production in my garden. I'm focused on a balance of visual enjoyment, food production, and pleasant time spent working in the garden. If the squash bugs want my plant, I'd rather remove the host plant and hopefully reduce populations by eliminating their food source than smash and spray and still have a sickly looking plant. I can grow zucchini again next year, most likely a resistant variety, in a different area, perhaps planting a little later in the season, and hope that the squash bugs leave it alone.

Maybe this sounds a little too passive, and I should fight harder for my plants. I don't mean to sound complacent or as if my garden isn't worth the fight. That's not it at all. It's just that if an insect or disease comes to my garden, something is out of balance. I need to figure out what that imbalance is and correct it. If that means pulling out a plant for the season, figuring out what may have gone wrong, and trying again next year, then that is what I do. In my squash bug example, it is important to do a little homework and try to understand where the pests came from, why they attacked, and what I might do to prevent it next time.

There are many factors that can make a plant weakened and prone to attack. If I don't understand what those factors are, if I react by spraying to kill the attacker, that is not sustainable. Sometimes the imbalance may be water—too much or too little. It may be the nutrients in my soil or the pH of the soil. It may be that I have planted the same plant (or the same family of plant) in the same spot for too many years and disease has built up or insect pests have made a home in the soil near that plant. Many times, if a plant is healthy, it can withstand attack from a pest, and the result is often only cosmetic, like flea beetle holes in arugula. Chances are, if the arugula is healthy and large enough, the flea beetles won't do enough damage to kill it, and it will be a little lacy looking for a while until the beetles move on.

This is not to say that I won't make any effort to control pests in my garden. I spend a lot of time out there, and while I'm there I pay attention. If I see a problem, I'll make an effort to understand it and determine if action is warranted. If I see a couple of Japanese beetles, I will fill a bucket with soapy water and flick them off the plant into the drink, because I have found that doing this for a few minutes a day for about a week seems to take care of the problem. But to set up a regimen of constantly battling pesky critters to save a few squash or tomatoes, while the plant looks progressively worse for the wear, I don't see much value in it. I will try again next year, maybe with a different plant combination in a different area. In the meantime, I'll fill that spot with some easy and fast-growing plant like chard or kale, so I have something productive and attractive growing there for the rest of the season. And I also take note throughout the season of the plants that do well and that don't need a lot of protection, and plant more of those the next year.

If I were growing large numbers of plants to sell for my livelihood, well, that would be a different story. I would take much greater precautions and probably employ some organic control methods. But on the scale of a garden that is primarily for pleasure, I do not wish to spend my time in battle. Rather, I watch, I learn, and I understand. Armed with that understanding, I try again next year.

MORE REASONS TO GROW OUR OWN FOOD

Despite the cost of seeds, supplies, water, and my own labor, it always feels to me like I get from my garden so much more than I put into it. And when I can go an entire summer without having to shop for many vegetables, herbs, and fruit, I do feel like I'm saving money. I've never actually done the math, and frankly I don't want to, because the benefits I find from growing my own food far outweigh the expenditures. Even if I found that it would be cheaper to buy all my produce from the market, I would still grow my own because what I get from it goes far beyond anything having to do with money. Where else but in a garden can you get good exercise, have time to think, enjoy the outdoors, learn, and come away with armloads of food?

Countless perks come with growing your own food, no matter how or where you do it. If you have ever grown any of your own food, you know the excitement of growing interesting, unusual varieties and the fulfillment that comes from bringing fresh food right from your garden to your table.

Flavor of course is a big part of the equation too. There's something different about the flavor of a tomato or zucchini that you plucked right out of your own garden. There's a magical sweetness that comes with the knowledge that your hard work and care helped these plants grow from tiny seeds into lush, bountiful plants. Nothing can quite compare to the singular flavor of a cherry tomato picked from the vine with the warmth of the sun still lingering in the juices, nor the delicate snap of a just-picked bean or the perfect tenderness of salad greens right out of the garden. These flavors are what drive so many of us to spend hours on our knees tending and pampering, staining our fingernails with soil. The promise of real food—sweet, rich, nutritious food—tasting of the sun.

A landscape filled with food and flowers is a delight for the entire family. In this late-summer raised bed, the irises have long since bloomed, but the tapestry of green makes it all the more exciting to discover a patch of sweet raspberries ready to be picked.

LOOKING AT EDIBLES IN A NEW WAY

There's something wonderful and surprising when you take these delicious, bountiful plants and place them into the realm of the ornamental landscape. Suddenly they take on new life, new purpose. Not only do they provide food, but they add color, texture, and form to your landscape.

It's all in the way we look at the plants. We've been trained all our lives to think of vegetables having a place only in a vegetable garden. Period. Why is that? Why are these plants considered so different from those we choose to put in our flowerbeds? Food plants have color, flowers, interesting forms, and textures. Why then do we force them into tight rows? If you're going to grow food in your yard, why not make it look nice? You're going to look at it every single day and likely spend a good bit of time out there. It doesn't take much more planning or work, and you'll be treated with a garden that does it all.

A pepper becomes much more than just a pepper when you take a fresh look and see the plant for its structural beauty, and the individual fruits for their sleek shape and eye-catching colors.

A delicious sight when coming or going, this rustic raised bed just outside the door is filled with herbs, perennials, and annuals. Containers of tomatoes and eggplant sit on the wall of the bed, placing everything within a few steps of the kitchen.

emily's 10 favorite
edibles
• • • • • •

These ten veggies, fruits, and herbs are my favorites to grow in the landscape. Each one has a slightly different combination of ease, visual interest, and deliciousness. There are choices here for sunny and shady spots in the yard and options for any climate. They're easy enough for a novice and yet offer challenging options to satisfy the creative, well-seasoned gardener.

Alpine strawberry

Blueberry

Celery

Chard

Eggplant

Kale

Mizuna mustard

Parsley

Tomato

Zucchini (bush-type)

ABOVE: When you think of plants like cabbage and strawberries, think not only about the food they provide but the distinct colors and textures they might add to the landscape. The glossy, deep green, serrated leaves of the strawberry contrast nicely with the broad, fleshy, silver-blue leaves of the cabbage.

AT RIGHT: If you're looking for more color in the garden, seek out varieties like 'Ruby Red' Swiss chard. The crimson stalks and deep burgundy leaves are just as striking as the ornamental cannas in the background.

A NATURAL BALANCE

A successful garden is all about balance. A balance of flowers, fruits, veggies, and herbs creates a diverse ecosystem in your yard. Growing edibles and ornamentals together provides benefits above and beyond aesthetics and food. The mere intermingling of a wide variety of plants makes for a healthier, and therefore more easily managed, garden. You've heard how mono-cropping in large-scale agriculture is detrimental because planting only one crop leads to nutrient depletion, disease incidence, and insect pest problems, meaning huge losses if there's a problem. Planting so much of one crop means that if a pathogen or insect finds one plant it likes, it's bound to find all the rest—and that's not good for yields.

That's why diversified farming is such a good idea. Having a mixture of plants means risk and nutrient needs are spread out among a lot of different crops. So if an insect pest attacks one

This wild relative of the potato is seen in one of its natural ranges in the Peruvian Andes. Like most plants in their native habitats, it grows in a community with many other plants that share and contribute resources. ERIC TEPE PHOTO

crop, chances are most other crops will be okay and make up for that loss. By not being dependent solely on one crop, chances for success are higher. When it comes to nutrients, there are heavy feeders like cucumbers that take up a lot of nutrients from the soil as they grow, and there are generous nutrient-providers like beans that actually give back to the soil. There are sun-worshipping squash that demand the brightest spot in the yard, and there are easygoing greens that'll take whatever bit of sun is left over. There are pest-sensitive plants that might be severely damaged by insects or disease, and there are plants that help ward off pests or attract pest enemies.

These theories apply similarly on the small-scale home landscape. A diverse planting also means lots of food for pollinators and other beneficial insects, which are essential to any farm or garden. The more good insects we can attract the better off our plants will be. It is the balance of this natural give and take, which is inherent in naturally occurring ecosystems, that we should try to achieve in our yards and gardens. This balance is part of what makes this type of gardening so logical, fascinating, beautiful, and ultimately successful.

KEEPING TRACK

It's a great idea to keep notes of all that happens in your garden. From the very beginning phase of studying your site, to amending the soil, to planning the design and choosing plants, and all through the season, including pest and disease incidence, weather events, plant performance, and even harvest details. A garden notebook is a great way to collect and organize this information. This could be a virtual notebook organized on a computer or a good old-fashioned three-ring binder filled with information you find in various places and notes that you keep throughout the season. I prefer the old-fashioned method because, for me, it's more inspiring to assemble and look through actual pages and pictures than to click through folders and image files. Either way, the garden notebook is a valuable tool that you can build to suit your interests. It's a place to keep details about various plants, ideas you'd like to try, sketches of your garden plans, calendars for seed starting and transplanting, and notes from throughout the season. My notebook has various tabbed sections of all this information and also a chronological journal for notes. It helps me plan for subsequent years, with notes of which plant combinations worked well, which didn't, and so on. It's a pleasant task to sit down in the evening and jot a few notes about what's been happening in the garden, like the day I spotted a praying mantis, when I noticed a collection of squash bug eggs on the underside of a zucchini leaf, or on what date I harvested the first juicy-ripe tomato.

Your garden notebook is the perfect place to keep notes, sketches, photos, ideas, and growing information. It can be as personal as a scrapbook or as simple as a file on your computer. Either way it will help you plan your garden and serve as a record for each season's details. MODESIGNS58/ISTOCKPHOTO

success is
in the details

The planning phase can be one of the most exciting parts about landscaping with food plants. Imagining what your garden will look like, planning the layout, choosing plants, and deciding where they'll go is exciting and often the part I most look forward to every year as I update, alter, and renew my plans. But before any of that, it is important to take a few steps to understanding what you are working with. Whether you're starting from scratch or adding a few edibles here and there, you need to know a few things. This is an opportunity to get to know your yard intimately and take advantage of the best it has to offer your plants. Light, soil, moisture, and drainage are vital elements to gardening that can make or break your experience.

Visual interest doesn't have to come solely from color. A tapestry of green can delight the senses with variations in texture and scale by incorporating a multitude of leaf shapes, plant forms, and support structures. Trellised hops take center stage here.

EXISTING PLANTS

Chances are you are not starting with a completely empty yard, but have some existing plants, trees, and shrubs. These existing plants are helpful in planning your landscape by giving you anchors to work from. You may have a few well-placed trees or shrubs in the front yard that frame the house or a prized lilac or dogwood that you don't want to part with. And surely you shouldn't. These existing plants offer a starting point and make the job of choosing other plants easier than if you were starting with a completely empty yard.

GRASS

I love grass, so I'm not going to say you should rip out your lawn and fill the space with fruits and vegetables. On the contrary: A healthy lawn is a delight to see and feel. Grass brings calmness to a yard and is the perfect surface for kids to play, pets to run, and the rest of us to lounge. Grass also sets off garden beds nicely. A neat edging of grass along a garden bed makes a good contrast with the various textures and colors of the plants.

This yard has existing trees, shrubs, and perennials that help set the stage for some new edible plantings. Plants can simply be tucked in here and there, or existing beds can be enlarged to add even more plants.

A well-manicured lawn makes a yard inviting and creates the perfect backdrop for these beautiful limestone raised beds of raspberries, rhubarb, and irises.

Garden borders can be expanded to create beautiful curved beds. Here the soft transition from grass to garden unifies the look and provides easy access for this happy chicken in search of insects.

But, there is such a thing as too much grass. If you're finding you don't have the space to work edibles into your yard, take a look at how much grass you have. Does it go right up to the house? Right up to the fence or property line? Are these areas of grass useful? What if, instead of mowing grass right up to the fence, you had an undulating border of plants to soften that hard, straight line. By removing a few feet of grass on the edge of the yard, you could turn a virtually unused space into a beautiful, productive border filled with flowers, fruit, vegetables, and herbs.

In the front yard you may have a walkway to the house that cuts through the center of the lawn. Break up the monotony by breaking up some of that grass, widening the garden bed that runs along the front of the house, and bringing it down along the path. You'll add a lot of space for edibles and create a much more welcoming, inviting entry.

LIGHT

Most food-producing plants prefer six or more hours of sunlight per day. Sun-lovers like tomatoes and peppers do better with eight hours or more. This may be hard to come by on an urban street with lots of big old trees. If this sounds like your yard and you're hoping to grow some edibles, you may need to be strategic about where in your yard you choose to do it. If you already have some flourishing garden beds that get plenty of light, then work in some edibles there. Keep some of those ornamentals though, for diversity.

If you don't have any garden beds yet, take a good look at your yard at different times of day and keep track of where the light moves and how long each area is in the sun. This is one of the most important steps in creating a successful garden or landscape of any kind. You have to know how light travels through your yard, how much of a shadow is cast by that ancient spruce on the corner, and where the shadow moves during the day. Otherwise your plants will struggle, and you'll likely spend years trying to make up for it with fertilizers and other things that won't work. Plants need light. They need light to make the energy they use to grow. Things like tomatoes need a lot of light because it takes a lot of energy to create big, juicy, flavorful fruits.

Not only is the amount, or duration, of light important, but so is the quality and intensity of the light. A spot that gets six hours of morning sun is going to be different from a spot that gets six hours of afternoon sun. Both of these are considered full sun, but the afternoon sun is hotter than the morning sun and will be a bit much for many plants. In an afternoon-sun spot, plant a few heat-lovers like okra, collards, malabar spinach, hot peppers, and cucumber. In the

TOP: Dappled light is broken up light coming through the leaves of trees. This can be a good place for greens or root vegetables that can tolerate a little shade.

BOTTOM: Full shade is a tough spot for most edibles, and these areas are best left to shade-loving ornamentals. However, the diminutive alpine strawberry will grow happily in the shade and offer tiny sweet berries to the gardener.

OPPOSITE PAGE: Here's the beauty of edible landscaping: instead of choosing one spot to grow your "vegetable garden," you can work edibles in here and there where the light is best suited to them.

By taking some time to watch how light travels through your yard and keeping track of the hours the light is in certain areas, you'll discover how much light different areas receive and determine which plants will do best in which areas.

Shaded places are tricky for growing edibles. If the spot gets at least three hours of sun before plunging into shade, you may be able to coax a few edibles to grow. These nasturtiums even introduce a splash of color to an area where we might normally find monochromatic ornamentals such as hostas.

light: a rule of thumb

There's a general rule of thumb that can help you determine where to plant certain edibles in your yard. If the part you eat is the fruit of the plant (tomatoes, peppers, eggplant, beans, apples, cucumbers, zucchini, etc.) the plant needs eight or more hours of sunlight. If the part you eat is a root (beets, radishes, carrots) it can tolerate a little less light. Finally if the part you eat is a stem or leaf (celery, chard, lettuce, kale) the plant can generally handle slightly shady conditions.

Of course there are always exceptions: Many fruit plants for instance, in their native habitats are understory plants and so can survive in part shade to shade conditions. The caveat is that the fruit will be very small. If you've ever picked wild blueberries, you know they are tiny. Wild raspberries are usually strangely shaped and small. Wild strawberries are also very small. In fact, almost any food plant grown in shady conditions will be less vigorous than if it were grown in the sun. This is biology—plants need light to create the energy required to grow.

Low-light conditions can be used to your advantage, if considered carefully. Lettuce, for instance, can handle somewhat shady conditions. It will be smaller and less colorful than if it were grown in the sun, but it will have a longer season because the cool shade slows down its growth and delays flowering, or bolting. So if you want to reduce the vigor of a plant for a particular reason, you may consider giving it a little more shade than typically recommended.

morning-sun areas, plant tomatoes, zucchini, beans, strawberries, and eggplant.

Next we have dappled light. Dappled light is light filtered by tree branches and leaves. The quality of light coming through depends greatly on the density of the foliage. Generally, light filtered through tall trees is bright but less intense than full sun. These dappled places are perfect for greens, peas, root veggies, even raspberries or strawberries.

Finally, there's full shade. That is shade from a very dense tree, a building, anything that prevents direct sun from reaching the ground for the majority of the day. These places are tricky for growing edibles. If the spot gets at least three hours of sun before plunging into shade, you may be able to coax a few greens to grow or some alpine strawberries. Less sun than that, and you may be better off sticking with ornamentals like hostas and impatiens in those areas.

Most of us don't have an entire yard with ideal light conditions, and that's the beauty of edible landscaping. Instead of choosing one spot to grow your "vegetable garden," you can work edibles in here and there where the light is best suited to them: a tomato or two in the sunny perennial garden, a border of lettuces along the cool patio. With each year you can try different combinations and adjust placement of plants to make the most of the light you have.

TOPOGRAPHY

Have you ever noticed a spot in your yard that pools up in the rain and always seems to be soggy? Or an area that seems to need more water than anywhere else? Even on a small scale, topography plays a big part in planning a landscape because of the way it dictates how moisture moves through the soil. A low spot may mean the roots of the plants are sitting in water almost all the time. While water is good for the roots, too much water deprives the roots of oxygen and creates an environment inhospitable to beneficial microorganisms in the soil. Without those, most plants will decline and eventually die. Persistently wet areas might be best suited to wetland ornamentals, while edibles are kept to the better-drained areas of the yard.

A high, dry area will also cause some challenges, because plant roots might dry out quickly. This can generally be managed better than a low wet area, but it may mean excessive watering to keep roots from drying out. A thick layer of mulch on a high, dry planting area will help slow moisture movement and hold it in the soil longer. A dry area might be a good place for somewhat drought-resistant edibles like the Mediterranean herbs: oregano, thyme, sage, rosemary. These will need adequate water to get

established, but once they are, they can handle drier conditions. Chard and mustard greens would do okay in a dry area too. But to make it work for a nice combination of plants, water regularly and mulch well.

One solution to topography challenges is terracing. By constructing flat levels that step down a steep slope, the space is transformed from a difficult slope to multiple, flat planting areas. Terracing solves problems of erosion and improper drainage because the slope is eliminated. Terracing may initially be costly and time consuming, but the result is a planting area where before there was none.

SOIL

The soil. This is where the magic happens. Soil is made up of mineral particles, organic matter, air, water, and organisms. A balance of these various elements makes for ideal soil, but that is uncommon, especially in urban areas where compaction, contamination, and years of use are likely. Your yard may have light sandy soil, heavy clay soil, or something in between. Extremes of soil texture create challenges for gardeners. Clay soil is challenging because it is difficult to dig into and break up and is very slow to

Terracing is a great solution for a sloped yard. By creating flat terraces that step down the slope, water runoff and erosion are virtually eliminated. Flat planting beds make the perfect place for all kinds of edibles and ornamentals. Even the walls of the terrace can be utilized for containers and other decorative items.

Soil texture depends on the ratio of particle sizes in the soil. You can get a general idea of your soil texture by taking a handful of damp soil and squeezing it. If it sticks together in a firm, sticky ball, it's likely clay soil. If it doesn't stick together and crumbles apart, it's likely a sandy soil. If the soil holds together but isn't sticky, and crumbles a little when you squeeze it, it's a loam soil and is a good balance of the three particle sizes. Here is a rich, loam soil. JULIJA SAPIC/SHUTTERSTOCK

drain. A high proportion of sand creates a very gritty, light soil and can be challenging because sandy soil tends to drain too quickly and doesn't provide good structure for plant roots. Loam soil is a balance of particle sizes and is generally the best for gardening. Most gardeners, however, are not blessed with perfect loam soil in their yards and have to amend it to make the soil hospitable for plants. This is generally done over time and is best achieved by adding organic matter to the soil.

Soil can be somewhat mysterious, and it's hard to tell just by looking what kind of soil you have. Before doing any planting, it's a good idea to have a soil test done. This will help determine the amount of organic matter in the soil and many other useful details that will help you plan a successful garden.

ORGANIC MATTER

Organic matter and microorganisms in the soil help determine how the soil is held together. Organic matter comprises anything that used to be alive: plants, animals, microbes that are all in various stages of decay. Millions of unseen microorganisms, along with larger organisms like insects and worms, work symbiotically to break down the organic matter in the soil, which then contributes to soil structure, air and water movement, and nutrient recycling.

Organic matter in the soil is vital for lush, healthy plants. The more organic matter in the soil, the more active the microbes. The more active the microbes, the more nutrients are made available for plants, and the better the soil structure. The better the soil structure, the easier it is for air and water to move through and for

soil testing

Have you ever gone to the garden center looking for fertilizer and found yourself standing there staring at a confounding collection of bags and boxes with a dizzying array of numbers and recommendations? You might know what the letters on the bags mean: N-P-K for nitrogen, phosphorus, potassium, for example. But look at the rows of bags on the shelves and you'll see 10-0-0, 0-12-20, 15-15-15, 6-12-18...yikes. How to choose? Turn a bag around and start reading about macronutrients, micronutrients, acidity, alkalinity... holy smokes. How are you supposed to know what to get? Do you need any of it at all? The only one way to know for sure is to have your soil tested.

Search online for soil testing in your state and one of the first results will probably be a state university soil testing lab. Most I've come across have detailed instructions on how to take the samples, where to send them, and how to understand the results. After reading those, if you're still not sure, there are quite a few videos online produced by universities and garden centers that show step by step how to do it.

When you receive the results, usually in a couple of weeks, you'll learn the pH of your soil, which nutrients are high or low, and what might need to be added to get the soil ready for planting. At that point you can choose the type of product to use—organic, conventional, whatever works for you. By carefully following instructions, you'll be on your way to helping build healthy, balanced soil. Balanced soil means the soil is able to support not only plants but the millions of tiny organisms in the soil that are essential for plant health.

By having your soil tested every other year, you'll be able to take responsible steps toward maintaining healthy soil, instead of reacting and going for a quick fix, which is less productive and less sustainable in the long run.

Organic matter in the soil consists of all plant, animal, and microbial matter—anything that was alive at one time. Over time, these materials break down and contribute to rich, dark soil perfect for growing healthy plants.

Plants that aren't getting adequate nutrients often exhibit discoloration in the leaves (chlorosis). This blueberry leaf has signs of iron deficiency. This is common in blueberries planted in soils that have a pH that is too high. Blueberries thrive in acidic soils (low pH). High pH prevents the plant from absorbing nutrients.
AUTHOR PHOTO

plant roots to develop. Organic matter improves the soil's ability to accept, retain, and move water. It works somewhat like a sponge, attracting water and soaking it up, transferring it to the other sponge-like organic matter particles throughout the soil.

Soils that are used for growing a lot of plants might be lacking in organic matter. The plants we grow in the soil year after year use up the nutrients created by the small amount of organic matter that is naturally present. Therefore it's important to regularly add organic matter, generally in the form of compost. By amending the soil regularly with organic matter, the soil will literally come to life. All that activity will work over time to develop well-drained, nutrient-rich soil.

NUTRIENTS IN THE SOIL

Humans require nutrients to be healthy, and so do plants. Most gardeners are familiar with the major nutrients (macronutrients) plants need—nitrogen, phosphorus, and potassium—because they are the primary nutrients in most commercially available fertilizers: N-P-K. There are also many nutrients that plants require in smaller amounts to grow vigorously and be productive, known as micronutrients. Many of these are naturally available in the soil thanks to organic matter. But after consecutive years of growing plants in the soil, some of these nutrients are bound to be depleted. Because annual vegetables grow so quickly and take up nutrients

A well-planned front-yard garden can take a house from drab to extraordinary and make a welcoming statement to the neighborhood. Incorporate a variety of color and forms, keep everything tidy, pruned, pinched, trellised, and weed-free, and visitors will be surprised at just how fabulous a food garden can look.

in rather large amounts, areas of the garden planted primarily with these can become depleted quickly. That's one reason why combining many different plants is such a good idea—different plants use nutrients at different rates, and some even provide nutrients to the soil.

When soil nutrients are out of balance, strange things happen in the garden: leaves turn yellow, brown, or other unusual colors; leaves are misshapen; plants look wilted despite plenty of water; plants seem to stop growing; strawberries, tomatoes, and other fruits are strangely shaped. Often these are the result of nutrient deficiencies, but nutrients in excess can also cause some challenges.

Chances are, by planting a wide variety of edibles and ornamentals, annuals and perennials, trees and shrubs, you'll go a long way to creating and maintaining a balanced environment for your plants. Through regular additions of compost, cover-cropping, crop rotation, and the occasional application of a nutrient-boosting organic fertilizer, you're bound to have a healthy, vigorous, bountiful, and beautiful landscape.

CHAPTER **3**

creating the
edible landscape

Perhaps you already have garden beds established, in which case
you can focus your creative energy on which plants to choose and
where they'll go in your garden. But maybe you're starting from
scratch. Maybe you have a yard filled with grass, and you want to
replace some of it with colorful, delicious plants. In this case, you
can consider your yard a virtually blank canvas and start having
fun with bed shapes and paths, in addition to plant selection and
placement. If this is you, I consider you very fortunate because you
have a world of gardening possibilities at your fingertips.

**Kale is a great filler plant for the midground area of the garden. The
foliage provides a fairly neutral background for more colorful plants, and
it maintains its shape without any help from the gardener. Kale provides
the same service in containers.** SIMONE ANDRESS/SHUTTERSTOCK

You don't need a lot of space, or even a yard, to create something beautiful. And don't stop at the plants. This tiny urban balcony is thoughtfully designed with plants, containers, and furnishings with colors and textures that complement each other and maximize the usefulness and beauty of the space.

Either way, it's time to take a walk around your yard. Stop in different areas, look around, and imagine what your garden will be like. What do you see in your mind's eye? What shapes? What pathways? How do you imagine walking through? Do you see an entire yard bursting with color and flavor? A border along the fence? Perhaps a few beds here and there sprinkled with colorful lettuces? Stand in the doorway, front or back, and think about what you'd like to see as you step out. Maybe an entry garden along the front walk, welcoming guests with the scent of herbs, the sound of bees hovering around tomato blossoms. Take some time to ponder: How far do you want to go to pick a few fresh veggies for dinner? Do you relish the thought of walking all the way through a fragrant, colorful garden to get to your harvest, or would you rather be able to step right out the door and gather a few berries for your ice cream or a fresh tomato for your salad? Maybe both.

THE SIZE

The size of your garden will be determined by the size of your yard, the type of neighborhood you live in, and other needs the yard serves. A tiny urban lot may feel limiting, but you're only limited by your imagination and creativity. In fact, a small space can lead to exciting possibilities with vertical structures, raised beds, and containers. A very large space, a large suburban lot for example, can feel limiting in the sense that you may feel overwhelmed about where to start or how to organize and use the space well. The size of the space doesn't have to limit your creativity; rather it helps determine the scope and eventual design of your garden. The space you have to work with is one of the few predetermined elements of garden design and can definitely be used to guide your creativity.

By working within your constraints and re-imagining the space they define, you can create a visually interesting, practical, and productive yard. The great thing about this kind of gardening is the ability to pack a lot of variety into a small space. A few plants here and there can produce a season full of delicious food, especially if you choose varieties that produce continually throughout the season. Instead of traditional heading broccoli, for instance, you may choose a broccoli raab or rapini, which produce small sprouts similar to broccoli throughout much of the season, making the space they take up in the garden more efficient and productive than if it were only to produce one head of broccoli. What's more, these plants have a very interesting look and produce delicate yellow flowers once you're done harvesting.

This tree on a city street boulevard is surrounded by lettuce, tomato, cucumber, chard, and kale, along with a few zinnias and Stella d'oro lilies for color.

THE STYLE

Similar to the size of your garden, style may be somewhat determined by your home, neighborhood, existing landscape, or yard features. There's a good chance you are starting with some existing plantings, a patio or deck, or perhaps a fence around the yard. Any number of these things may speak to a certain style and guide your choices. Then again, you may decide to start completely fresh. Either way, this is your chance to figure out what style you want to create. Do you prefer regular, ordered shapes with lots of geometry? Or would something more natural and loose fit your personality, your house, your yard?

Be creative when seeking out areas to plant edibles in your yard. Don't stop at the obvious, showy areas. This quiet space behind the garage is the perfect spot for raspberries, squash, iris, echinacea, ornamental grasses, and more. This welcoming variety of plants transforms an otherwise unused area into a tranquil destination in the yard.

A free-form, casual garden style has some nice benefits. Because the plants are so highly mixed, you can get a lot of variety into a very small space. One plant of each species might be sufficient, depending on the size of the plant, the size of the space, and any cross-pollination requirements the species may have. Because there is no distinct order to the groupings of plants, this style also makes it easy to replace plants as they go out of season. For example, when the lettuces begin to bolt in the midsummer heat, you could easily work something else in to take their place without too much disruption. Or you could simply let other plants in the vicinity fill in those gaps.

A large space can be a little overwhelming, as it can be difficult to find a place to start. But here, a lovely mound in the middle of the yard catches the eye and abounds with corn, squash, potted blueberries, herbs, and ornamentals.

Some people prefer a bit more order in their yards, and that can be just as pleasing. Some homes dictate a greater formality of design, and are better served by symmetry and straight lines. This can be fun to create, and with the wide variety of interesting colors and textures that food plants provide, there's a wide range of possibilities. You do not need to limit yourself to yews or arborvitae to create well-shaped hedges and focal points. Rather, a row of currants could be trimmed to a formal hedge, and a pair of graceful plum trees could create an elegant frame for the front entry of a home. A geometrically planned design of herbs and flowers creates a peaceful order that allows the eyes and mind to rest, while distinctly swirling rows of alternating color lettuces following a path can be exciting and intriguing.

Whatever your style—casual, formal, or anywhere in between—you can create a gorgeous yard using a whole new range of interesting, colorful, and delicious plants.

EXPLORING PLANT OPTIONS

It can feel a little overwhelming when you first start looking through seed catalogs or making lists of the plants you want to include in your edible landscape. There are so many options that it can be difficult to narrow it down. Take tomatoes, as an example. You've got the heirlooms, which right there pose an enormous array of choices. The bizarre shapes and colors are so intriguing, not to mention the range of flavors. Add to this the hybrid varieties and the options increase exponentially. Determinate, indeterminate, cherry, grape, beefsteak, early-season, late-season. How do you choose?

The first thing to do is to sit down and make a list. Include in that list every fruit and vegetable you enjoy eating. If you're anything like me, this list will be quite long. Even if you think the plant might

An informally planted combination of edibles and ornamentals lends an air of ease to the garden. Clumps of plants in various colors, textures, and forms allow the features of each to shine. Single plants here and there, like the chard pictured, make a statement among the masses of alyssum, cosmos, borage, and flowering broccoli raab.

Gardening for small spaces may seem limiting, but the only true limitation is your imagination.

be hard to grow, or may not grow in your climate, add it to the list. There may be an option for growing a non-hardy plant in a container, or there may be a similar plant to use as an alternative. Write down everything you think of. There's time for editing later.

On the top of many lists will likely be tomatoes, lettuce, peppers, beans, cucumbers, and basil. These garden staples are common because they're relatively easy to grow, start easily from seed, produce a lot throughout the season, and are delicious fresh from the garden. Now stretch your imagination a bit. Think of going to the grocery store or farmers market. What are the foods

Straight lines and angles immediately give an air of formality. A few simple measurements and the aid of stakes and strings make layout of geometric patterns easy. The combination of plants you choose can take the design in many different directions. Try alternating colors of lettuces, or play with textures—stick straight chives and leafy greens like feathery red mizuna mustard on the right.

that catch your eye that you can never pass up when they're in season? Asparagus? Pie cherries? Brussels sprouts? Apples? Potatoes? Write them all down. If you need a little inspiration, page through a seed catalog or peruse one online. You'll undoubtedly be reminded of a few foods you like that you may have never thought of growing yourself, like artichokes, okra, or cranberries.

Don't stop at the edibles. Remember it's important to have lots of ornamentals in the edible landscape to add color and variety, attract insects, and generally keep the garden diverse and healthy. I tend to look for ornamentals that have a long bloom season, are notably good at attracting beneficial insects, and have great color. I also choose several of about three different sizes: low and trailing or mounding for borders, medium height for filling in the middle ground, tall and stately for backgrounds.

Kohlrabi is a unique and eye-catching addition to the landscape. When planning its placement, keep in mind its heavy texture and fully green color. A light textured and colorful plant like cosmos provides a good contrast in both texture and color. A trailing annual could be a good choice to help fill in the gaps after the kohlrabi is harvested.

Once you have that list completed, it's time to learn a little about these plants—their size, shape, color, light and other growing requirements, as well as each plant's USDA hardiness zones (if it's a perennial plant). This step is important because it'll help you narrow down which plants you can grow in your area and figure out where to put the plants in your garden to help them be productive and attractive. Remember, varieties will differ a bit, so if you have specific varieties in mind it will be helpful to find this information in catalogs or online. If you'll be starting a lot of your plants from seed, you'll have a choice of many varieties that are unique or highly ornamental. If you plan to buy most plants as seedlings from the garden center, you may have fewer varieties to choose from, but still plenty of options. Remember, as you plan your garden, you'll need to be flexible because the garden center won't always have the exact variety you had in mind. But you'll surely find something close that will work equally well. What will make it unique is how you put it all together in your yard.

It's important to determine the size, texture, form (growth habit), and color of the various plants you're planning to include in your landscape, just as you would if you were planting ornamentals. These details will help determine where the plants will fit into the landscape, whether or not they'll need to be supported, which other plants will grow well near them, as well as how the plant will look. For instance, if you'll be including tomatoes in your landscape, you'll need to know if the varieties you choose are determinate or indeterminate, because these two growth habits create quite different plants. Determinate tomatoes support themselves fairly well and may only need a simple stake to keep them upright when

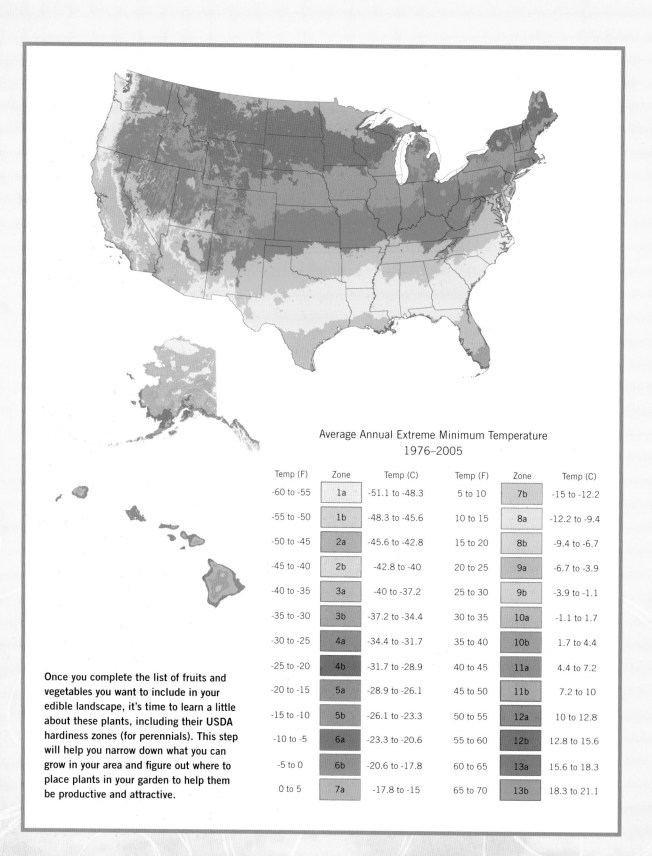

Average Annual Extreme Minimum Temperature
1976–2005

Temp (F)	Zone	Temp (C)	Temp (F)	Zone	Temp (C)
-60 to -55	1a	-51.1 to -48.3	5 to 10	7b	-15 to -12.2
-55 to -50	1b	-48.3 to -45.6	10 to 15	8a	-12.2 to -9.4
-50 to -45	2a	-45.6 to -42.8	15 to 20	8b	-9.4 to -6.7
-45 to -40	2b	-42.8 to -40	20 to 25	9a	-6.7 to -3.9
-40 to -35	3a	-40 to -37.2	25 to 30	9b	-3.9 to -1.1
-35 to -30	3b	-37.2 to -34.4	30 to 35	10a	-1.1 to 1.7
-30 to -25	4a	-34.4 to -31.7	35 to 40	10b	1.7 to 4.4
-25 to -20	4b	-31.7 to -28.9	40 to 45	11a	4.4 to 7.2
-20 to -15	5a	-28.9 to -26.1	45 to 50	11b	7.2 to 10
-15 to -10	5b	-26.1 to -23.3	50 to 55	12a	10 to 12.8
-10 to -5	6a	-23.3 to -20.6	55 to 60	12b	12.8 to 15.6
-5 to 0	6b	-20.6 to -17.8	60 to 65	13a	15.6 to 18.3
0 to 5	7a	-17.8 to -15	65 to 70	13b	18.3 to 21.1

Once you complete the list of fruits and vegetables you want to include in your edible landscape, it's time to learn a little about these plants, including their USDA hardiness zones (for perennials). This step will help you narrow down what you can grow in your area and figure out where to place plants in your garden to help them be productive and attractive.

Combining plants with contrasting growth habits, colors, and textures makes the most of the space and creates an attractive result. The vining habit of Malabar spinach allows it to climb vertically on a trellis, covering the support with its shiny deep green leaves, while silvery purple-blue cabbage fills the space beneath.

they become weighed down with big juicy tomatoes. Conversely, indeterminate tomatoes grow more like vines and do well on arbors, fences, or other trellises. Other plants can vary greatly in habit, depending on the variety, so be sure to know if your squash is trailing or bush-type, if your beans are runners or bush, if your pak choi is standard or dwarf, and whether or not your strawberries produce runners.

This is where a garden notebook comes in very handy. You can print out plant descriptions and photos from the Internet, or cut them out of seed catalogs and group them together in categories so they're easy to find. For example, a section on greens can include all kinds of lettuce, chard, kale, mustard, arugula, and so on. You could group them by size, so if you're looking for a short plant to add to a border you can page to that section and choose the right plant to fit the space. An online search can provide descriptions about the size, texture, and color of most plant varieties out there. You can track down growing information, often from university extension websites and seed company websites, and print that to include in the binder. An online image search can provide photos of the plant in different stages of growth and used in different ways (border, container, etc.). This information can be grouped on a page for inspiration and as a reminder of what the plant looks like. If a lot of varieties of a particular plant are available (tomatoes, lettuce, eggplant, etc.) print out info pages on several different varieties and add those to the binder. By doing all this, you will learn about the plants and become familiar with them and at the same time build a reference tool that you can go back to year after year.

CHOOSING PLANTS

When you have a long list of plants to choose from for your landscape, it can be tough to narrow the list down. There's one main factor that can help narrow down your list, and that is light.

Earlier in this book, I suggested you study the light in your yard, how it travels, and how much light certain areas receive in a day. By matching the plants with the light in your yard, you'll find you have a certain amount of space for various plants. Choose a few that you most want to try, and limit yourself to the space allowed.

The low-growing, twisting, blue-green foliage of German garlic chives (also known as curly chives) makes them a unique choice for borders in the ornamental food garden. The grassy foliage is the perfect foil for heavier-textured and deeply colored companions. The curly flower stalks produce lavender-pink blooms later in the season than most chive varieties.

Grading your plants from small in the front to tall in the back allows each to show off its best features, and you don't need a lot of space to get a lot of variation. Here low-growing, frilly marigolds hug the path and are a stunning contrast to the broad, fleshy leaves of white-fruited eggplant. Cucumbers climbing a trellis add more height in the rear of this narrow bed.

MATCHING PLANTS WITH LIGHT

Matching plants to the light in your yard is a fairly straightforward way to make some initial choices. Remember, most food-producing plants need six to eight hours of full sunlight to be vigorous and productive. By selecting the right plants for the right spot, you can maximize the sunny areas and also make use of the less sunny areas.

The Sun Lovers

If you only have a little bit of full sun in your yard, save this area for the sun-lovers. This is the spot for those heavenly tomatoes. Alongside your tomatoes, nestle in some basil, peppers, and eggplant. For a splash of color in sunny areas, achillea (yarrow) is one of my favorite perennials. While not edible, it is colorful, easy to grow and divide, and will attract myriad beneficial insects. Signet marigold, a small-flowered, mounding marigold, is a great choice for planting around the base of tomatoes, primarily because it creates a colorful base for those large, green plants. Petunias or other trailing annuals also work well around the base of taller plants. They fill the understory with color and may even help keep weeds away by filling in the empty space under tall plants.

Okra is another great choice for a sunny area. Okra is commonly thought to be a Southern plant, but that's not true. If started indoors in early spring, okra can be a wonderful plant in the northern landscape as well. Its creamy white or yellow hibiscus-like flowers give way to striking edible pods in colors from light green to deep burgundy. It's a beautiful and unusual plant that adds a lot of interest to the landscape.

Other favorites for the sunny spots are squash, cucumbers, strawberries, herbs, and melons. Strawberries can handle a little less sun, but a brilliant sunny spot will help them grow larger, healthier, and much more flavorful. Interplanted with bright, sun-loving annuals and perennials, all these plants will make the sunny places in your yard colorful, lush, and most of all . . . delicious!

A combination of tall, sun-loving eggplant, purple basil, and tomato offers some protection to low-growing signet marigold. The intense heat of the summer sun can cause signet marigolds to stop flowering, so planting them at the base of tall plants gives them a little reprieve. If flowering does slow down, fear not, for in the cooler days of autumn they'll start flowering again.

north meets south corner

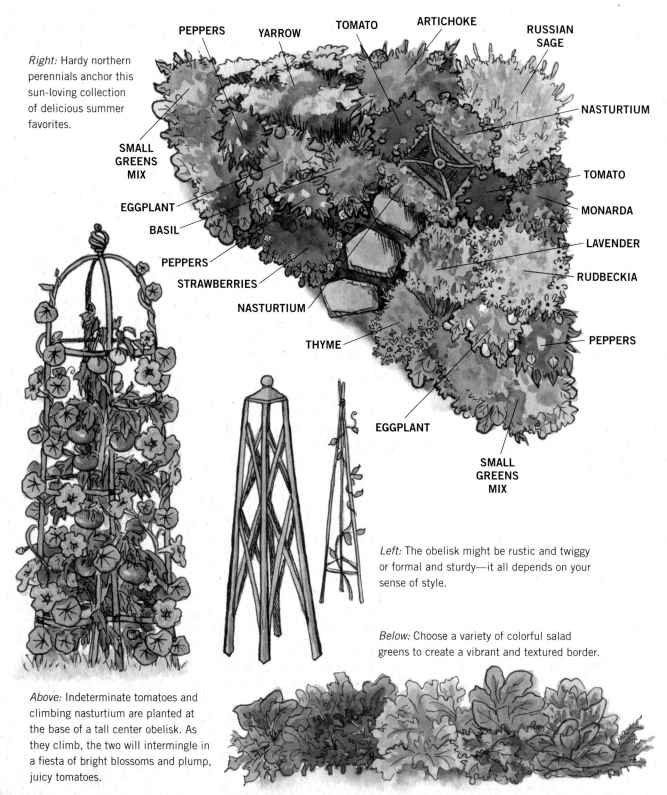

Right: Hardy northern perennials anchor this sun-loving collection of delicious summer favorites.

PEPPERS

YARROW

TOMATO

ARTICHOKE

RUSSIAN SAGE

NASTURTIUM

SMALL GREENS MIX

TOMATO

EGGPLANT

MONARDA

BASIL

LAVENDER

PEPPERS

RUDBECKIA

STRAWBERRIES

NASTURTIUM

THYME

PEPPERS

EGGPLANT

SMALL GREENS MIX

Left: The obelisk might be rustic and twiggy or formal and sturdy—it all depends on your sense of style.

Below: Choose a variety of colorful salad greens to create a vibrant and textured border.

Above: Indeterminate tomatoes and climbing nasturtium are planted at the base of a tall center obelisk. As they climb, the two will intermingle in a fiesta of bright blossoms and plump, juicy tomatoes.

ILLUSTRATIONS BY CHANDLER O'LEARY (ANAGRAM-PRESS.COM)

companion planting and interplanting

Companion planting is one of those concepts that tends to result in crinkled brows when you mention it to a horticultural scientist. And rightly so. Much of the information available on companion planting isn't based on solid science, but rather assumptions and tradition. And while that's not all bad, it is hard to give sound advice if it's not backed up with some kind of factual information. For example, it's pretty much standard gardener knowledge that you should plant marigolds near your tomatoes, but do you know why? Probably not, but everyone does it because of the lore. (Actually, this one does have some scientific basis—some species of marigolds planted near tomatoes have been shown to reduce damage by root-knot nematodes.) Should the marigolds be planted around the tomatoes as some sort of barrier? Or planted between them? How close? Do only certain varieties work? Try to find the answers to these questions and you'll find a dizzying array of conflicting advice. I'm not sure anyone knows for sure. There's been surprisingly little research done on the subject, and the research that has been done is generally inconclusive.

The idea behind companion planting is that certain plants, when growing near each other, can offer benefits to each other to promote vigor, repel pests, or improve productivity. There are a lot of different reasons why this would work. Some plants add nutrients to the soil. Some plants have natural pest-deterring characteristics. Conversely, some plants create an environment that may prove hostile to any plants around it. The idea of companion planting is reasonable, but it can be difficult to pin down these effects strictly to plant combinations without an extremely controlled environment. There are so many things going on in the soil and in the environment around those plants that a combination of millions of individual factors can cause plants to flourish or fail, making an extremely controlled environment for studies like this very difficult to establish.

My advice on the subject is to give it a try. What have you got to lose? It is interesting to set up little experiments in the garden to see how some of the combinations work. The major benefit of companion planting, as I see it, is the overall diversity it brings to the garden through interplanting. If you mix up your crops, planting many kinds of flowers and herbs among your veggies and fruits, chances are your plants will do well for a number of reasons. By combining plants of different families you eliminate large expanses of single crops. Since pests are generally crop-specific, this helps limit pest damage to a small area, one or two plants, instead of an entire bed of that plant. This goes for insect pests as well as diseases. Soil-borne diseases may not pose as much of a threat in a highly diversified garden as they would in a large mono-crop setting, because the host plants for particular diseases are separated by lots of other non-host plants. And if you practice rotation, you'll likely be even more successful in outsmarting pesky soil-borne diseases. While fending off pests by interplanting, you'll also be inviting lots of beneficial insects and other helpful creatures into your garden, presenting them with a wide variety of food sources and shelter: all good things.

Easygoing Part-Sun Plants

Thankfully there are quite a few plants that don't need to worship the sun quite as much as the tomato, that are more than happy to relax in a bit of shade now and then. These plants are the mainstay of any edible landscape, offering color, texture, and interest with an undemanding nature. Greens make up the majority of this group, and of the greens, chard is one of the best for its range of colors, easiness to grow, and many uses in the kitchen.

Kale and other greens are fabulous additions to the less-sunny parts of the landscape and great in the kitchen as well. The many varieties of kale offer a rainbow of color and interesting leaf shapes and textures for your garden. The leaves range in color from blue-green to purple-red, all with a silver-gray tinge that makes them a great backdrop to brightly colored annuals and perennials.

TOP RIGHT: Kale, broccoli raab, and calendula are easy-to-grow plants that will tolerate a bit of shade. The vibrant colors and varying textures and forms make these three attractive garden companions.

BOTTOM RIGHT: Swiss chard is easy to grow and makes a stunning addition to any area of the garden. Harvest often to keep the plants looking their best. Simply cut off a few outer leaves about an inch from the base. NORMAN CHAN/SHUTTERSTOCK

OPPOSITE PAGE: Lettuces happily grow in the dappled shade of taller plants, such as beans growing on a teepee. Red leaf and multicolored varieties are readily available and grow quickly from seed, making it easy for any gardener to add a pop of color to the garden and to the salad bowl. AUTHOR PHOTO

Mizuna mustard has a delicately fringed leaf and a low, mounded form, making it perfect for borders where it can be easily accessed. Pick young, tender leaves for salads, or use larger leaves to lend bright flavor to a stir-fry. KIMIKO SUZAKI/ISTOCKPHOTO

Kale is also very nutritious and can be used in salads, soups, sautés, and more.

Lettuces, mustard greens, arugula, and all kinds of baby greens add sparks of color to the landscape all throughout the season, especially if they're kept out of the heat of full sun.

All of the lettuces and small greens are fun to use as border plants, and thanks to the various colors and leaf textures available they can be a great edible alternative to annual ornamental bedding plants. Or better yet, they can be combined with ornamentals for an even more spectacular effect. It's fun to design with the rainbow of lettuce colors in the garden, and stunning effects can be created by sowing seeds of various colors of lettuce in intricate patterns.

Arugula and Mizuna mustard are two more attractive small greens. Arugula is a nice neutral green to grow with brighter-colored plants, and its peppery flavor spices up summer salads. Mizuna mustard has a unique leaf shape and brings great feathery texture to borders and beds. Its mounded form makes it great for borders. It's even nice when it bolts, because the tiny yellow flowers attract all kinds of pollinators.

The plants I mentioned here are a few of my very favorites to grow in my landscape. Beginning with a few of these interesting and delicious plants, and giving them the proper light, will get you started on your way to a beautiful edible landscape. There are countless others, and you can find details on those in the Appendix and other charts in the back of this book.

Lettuce is satisfyingly easy to grow and grows quickly. Within a few short weeks after planting the seeds tender leaves are ready for spring salads. Leaf lettuces are available in an endless range of colors and textures, and they're great in the landscape because you can pick a little at a time and they'll keep growing. TINYDEVIL/SHUTTERSTOCK

not-so-sunny border

Four or five hours of sun will suffice for a garden filled with greens and plants with woodland relatives. Even gooseberries and currants will be satisfied, though they might produce a little less fruit.

PEAS OR BEANS

CULVER'S ROOT

GOOSEBERRY

CURRANT

GOLDENROD

REDBOR KALE

RUSSIAN RED KALE

BROCCOLI RAAB · VIOLA · MONARDA · SKYBLUE ASTER · CHARD · CHIVE · LETTUCES · CELERY · ALPINE STRAWBERRIES · MONARDA

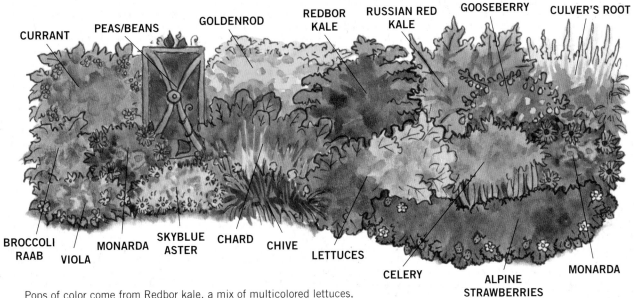

CURRANT · PEAS/BEANS · GOLDENROD · REDBOR KALE · RUSSIAN RED KALE · GOOSEBERRY · CULVER'S ROOT

BROCCOLI RAAB · VIOLA · MONARDA · SKYBLUE ASTER · CHARD · CHIVE · LETTUCES · CELERY · ALPINE STRAWBERRIES · MONARDA

Pops of color come from Redbor kale, a mix of multicolored lettuces, and of course chard—in your choice of pink, yellow, orange, or red. Banish straight lines to make the garden feel larger and more natural. An undulating edge is soft and welcoming, and allows plants to take on a natural shape.

ILLUSTRATIONS BY CHANDLER O'LEARY (ANAGRAM-PRESS.COM)

DESIGN: PUTTING IT ALL TOGETHER

By now you've spent some time in your yard imagining and envisioning. You also have a list of plants you would like to include in your edible landscape and a general idea of where the plants should go based on how much light they need. Now's the time to start putting it all together.

Designing a landscape takes into account a lot of variables, which can seem overwhelming at times. But a few basic guidelines can help you sort things out. And the great thing about plants is, if you don't like where they are one year you can plant them in a different spot next year. The flexibility of gardening is one of my favorite aspects. Each year I learn something new: that a particular plant does well in a certain area; that I like the way two plants look together; or conversely that two particular plants don't look so great together, and so on. It's all a learning process, which is part of what makes it so fun. Another part I love is seeing what I've planned in my mind and on paper begins to take shape as the growing season progresses.

The Basic Landscape Design Tips sidebar on pages 62–63 covers some of the textbook elements of creating a well-designed landscape. This might help you think about things you hadn't considered before such as visual balance, proportion, flow, and unity. The most important part, however, is simply to have a plan. Planning ahead takes out a lot of the guesswork and eliminates the haphazard placement of plants without regard to how they look with other plants around them.

If starting from scratch, it's time to get out pencil and paper. If you have an architect's plan drawing of your house and lot, you may want to make some copies to use as your base plan. Otherwise you can simply take some measurements of your house and your yard and do a basic scale drawing on a piece of graph paper. Or, faster still, find a satellite image of your house online, print it, and trace it on a piece of white paper. This isn't as hard as it sounds, and it will make planning much easier. Once you make your basic drawing, make several copies so you can sketch at will.

Working on the blank drawing of your yard, start with some rough sketches of planting beds, paths, sitting areas, anything you'd like to include in your landscape. These don't have to be works of art, just simple shapes on a page to help you visualize what you could create out of the space you have. One of the great parts about sketching these ideas is that you start to see your yard in a whole new light. For instance, the shape of the deck—or more importantly, the shapes of the planting spaces created where the deck meets the house. Or maybe you never realized that the thin strip of grass in the side yard gets the most sunlight of anywhere else in your yard and that it could perhaps be more than a connection between the front and the back yards. Details you may not have considered before start to become apparent. Force yourself to look beyond the obvious, and create several different versions of how you might lay out garden beds in your yard. It's easy to come up with one idea and settle for it, but it is exciting to push beyond that initial plan and try something totally different. Taking the time to get a good sense of your yard and play with different ideas helps you stretch your imagination and surprise yourself with unexpected creativity.

As you're sketching ideas, try to shoot for at least three versions of your plan. The first will incorporate the initial ideas that pop into your head. Then, by letting the mind and pencil wander, other options will materialize. You'll find that different bed shapes, paths, angles, and curves will change the entire feel of the space. Don't limit yourself. Have fun and go a little wild. A crazy idea might turn out to be exactly right for your yard. After you've sketched a few contrasting ideas, you can combine elements that will work well together and finally sketch up your master plan.

When getting started with this kind of planning, there are a few landscape elements to keep in mind that help guide the design, especially when starting from scratch. They are equally valuable when working in a few edibles here and there, because these elements help to define the space of the garden, provide visual interest, and create permanent structure in the garden that will help to provide a background for annual plants.

Try sketching multiple ideas for a basic garden layout: you're bound to see your yard in a whole new light. Play around with various shapes for garden beds and paths to make the most out of the space you have. You'll be surprised how dramatically the space can be transformed.
FOXY/SHUTTERSTOCK

fruit lover's front walk

PLUM

PEACH

CHERRY

Try to find dwarfing or semi-dwarfing fruit trees. These will not take up as much room in your yard, and their small size will make them easy to care for. Remember to prune every year to keep the trees healthy, productive, and looking good.

Try planting three similar dwarf fruit trees together in one large hole, angling the trees slightly outward, to make the most of a small space. Many fruit trees require pollen from a different variety to ensure good fruit set. You could plant three apple varieties, three cherry varieties, or even a plum, a peach, and a cherry. Check with the nursery to be sure the three you purchase have compatible pollen.

GRAPE

RASPBERRIES

LAVENDER

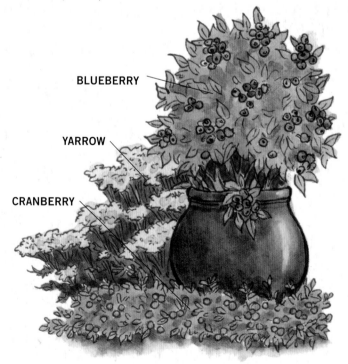

BLUEBERRY

YARROW

CRANBERRY

Long-blooming perennials help attract pollinators to the garden. They'll visit the fruit flowers too, ensuring pollination and good fruit set.

ILLUSTRATIONS BY CHANDLER O'LEARY (ANAGRAM-PRESS.COM)

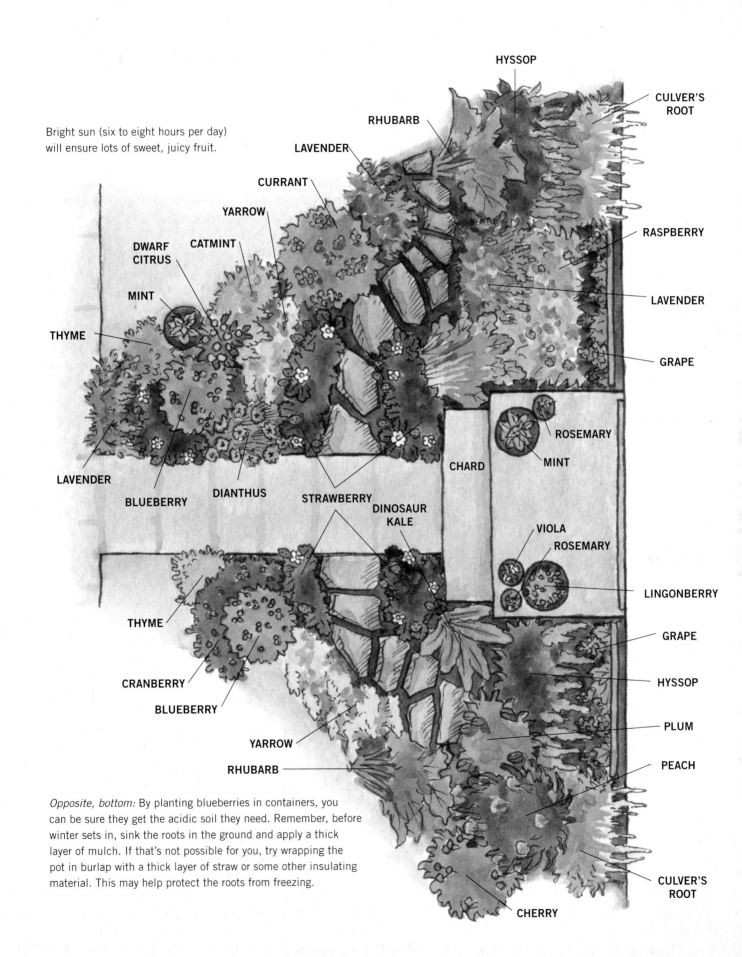

HYSSOP

CULVER'S ROOT

RHUBARB

LAVENDER

Bright sun (six to eight hours per day) will ensure lots of sweet, juicy fruit.

CURRANT

YARROW

RASPBERRY

DWARF CITRUS

CATMINT

LAVENDER

MINT

THYME

GRAPE

ROSEMARY

MINT

CHARD

VIOLA

ROSEMARY

LAVENDER

BLUEBERRY

DIANTHUS

STRAWBERRY

DINOSAUR KALE

LINGONBERRY

GRAPE

THYME

HYSSOP

CRANBERRY

PLUM

BLUEBERRY

PEACH

YARROW

RHUBARB

Opposite, bottom: By planting blueberries in containers, you can be sure they get the acidic soil they need. Remember, before winter sets in, sink the roots in the ground and apply a thick layer of mulch. If that's not possible for you, try wrapping the pot in burlap with a thick layer of straw or some other insulating material. This may help protect the roots from freezing.

CULVER'S ROOT

CHERRY

basic landscape design tips

Let's take a look at some basic design rules. First we want to look at design in a broad sense—the entire yard or the garden bed. These are the elements that apply to how the garden looks as a whole. Among these concepts, and the ones I pay most attention to are:

Simplicity

Balance

Proportion

Flow

Unity

The first thing I always think of when planning a design for a new garden or area of a garden is simplicity. By keeping the overall plan simple, the garden will be easy on the eye and a delightful, peaceful place to spend time. Simplicity might mean a couple of larger beds rather than a lot of little, complex-shaped beds running here and there with paths snaking through everywhere. Simplicity might mean one type of path material—brick or stone or grass, but not all three. Simplicity might mean starting out with one or two choice specimen plants instead of a wide variety of fruit trees, weeping ornamentals, evergreens—anything that caught your eye at the garden center. Start simple, start small, and work into it slowly, gradually building up the garden each year. It's difficult to know how much work this endeavor is going to take, so start simple to be sure you can handle it.

Balance can be a tricky concept to put into words, but we can all feel balance when we see it—or rather, we can all feel imbalance when we see it. Balance doesn't have to mean symmetry. Yes, symmetry is balanced, but balance can be attained through asymmetry as well. It comes down to visual weight. Two large trees on opposite sides of a house would certainly be symmetrical and balanced, but a large tree on one side of a house with little or no plantings around it might very well be balanced on the opposite side by a large bed planted with a variety of shrubs, small trees, and other plants. The mass of that grouped planting balances out the large tree on the other side. Balance can also be achieved in an asymmetrical design through repetition—of color, texture, size (concepts we'll get to below). When similar plants appear throughout a design they also help to provide visual balance.

Proportion refers to the sizes of elements in the garden and how they relate to each other. This one is pretty straightforward. A forty-foot pear tree would likely not look right in front of a tiny bungalow, just as a dwarf apple tree would not be at home in front of a three-story Victorian. The scale would be off. This applies to garden beds, path materials, and fencing as well. The size of your home and yard sets the scale of your garden. If you have an expansive yard, a couple of tiny

garden beds would probably not feel right, nor would a huge timber arbor seem fitting in a small urban lot.

Flow is how the eye, and the feet for that matter, moves through the garden. A lot of little disjointed garden beds that require a lot of walking to get to don't flow together as would two organically shaped beds separated by a gentle path of grass and balanced by a smooth swath of lawn. Think about how you want to move through your garden, what you would like to see from various vantage points in the yard. Choose plants that will catch the eye and draw you in, shapes that invite, repetition of forms or colors to pull the eye through.

All of the concepts above contribute to unity. A unified design is calming to the eye, feels grounded and connected to the space and the buildings around it, and has a consistent theme. Simplicity is key to unity. Employing a small variety of materials helps develop a sense of unity, as a small number of forms, textures, and colors are repeated throughout the garden. Too many different plants scattered here and there can become visually busy, and the eye will not have a place to rest. Having a style in mind as you get started will help you create a unified design, guiding your choices of plants, path materials, and so on.

When choosing plants, there are a few other design elements to keep in mind as well. These will help you reach the broader design goals above.

It is the relation of these qualities of a plant with others that matters, as the qualities may change when certain plants are paired:

Size

Form, or growth habit

Color

Texture

Size is fairly straightforward and is similar to the concept of proportion as discussed earlier. Here, however, we're talking about individual plants. The size of a plant and how it relates to that of a plant near it will contribute to proportion, flow, and balance. A tall plant next to a very short plant will not appear right, whereas a gradual gradation of size from tall to short will feel more natural and ease the eye through the garden.

Form refers to the growth habit and therefore shape of the plant. Is it upright, vase-shaped, rounded, creeping, vining? The form will help you determine where a plant should be placed and what other plants it might work well with. Several vase-shaped plants in a mass will leave gaps near the base, so a low, mounding plant would work nicely to fill that space. The contrast of forms is a fun thing to experiment with in the garden. How do rounded plants look against a backdrop of tall, upright plants? What other shapes look interesting together and accentuate each other. Which don't

work and look messy? Using pictures of plants can be a good way to play around with this idea.

Color is key in the garden and is one of the first things to catch the eye. Large masses of color have a striking visual effect, while small splashes of color here and there can help to unify. In a mixed garden, there is likely to be a lot of green. The use of color to break up the green and draw the eye through the garden can be very effective. Try not to go too crazy with color though. A little goes a long way, and too many different colors tend to become busy and un-unified. Stick to a few hues, and change it up a little every year for something new. One year, perhaps go with cool colors, with a few pops of warmth here and there. The next year, try it the other way around. Or perhaps you might choose white as your primary hue, with a glimmer of color where the tomatoes or eggplant peek through their foliage.

Texture is my favorite element to experiment with. Texture is a very relative concept, and a plant's texture is highly determined by the other plants around it. A plant may look coarsely textured next to one plant, but finely textured compared to another. It is this relativity that makes texture so much fun. A coarse-textured plant might have very broad, thick, fleshy leaves, or perhaps heavy, rough stems. Its broad leaves might be prickly, or smooth and dark. A finely textured plant likely has thin stems and slender leaves. Probably

a lot of space is visible between the stems and leaves. When coarse and fine textured plants, and those that fall somewhere in between, are combined, the textures play off of each other and draw attention to the contrasting features of each plant. Combining many plants of the same texture can have an interesting effect, but somewhere a contrast will be needed to help break up the continuity and move the eye along.

There's a lot more that one could delve into as far as design concepts are concerned, but these are some of the basics that you might keep in mind while planning your garden, choosing trellises, and picking out plants. You may not always get it right, and sometimes you might see the result and wonder what you were thinking. But that is the great thing about designing a garden: you can try things out and see how they go. You're bound to learn what looks good together and what doesn't, what unity feels like, how to create balance. It's all about trial and error. The more you try, the more you will refine what works and what doesn't. By keeping notes on these concepts as the garden progresses through the season, you'll develop a guide for new things to try next year and for years to come.

PATHS

A path is like an invitation into the soul of the garden. There's something wonderfully calming and fulfilling about stepping along a path through the heart of your plants, becoming surrounded by the color and fragrance of all that life. From this perspective, the sights and sounds and smells of the garden are all the more distinct: the hum of happy insects feasting on nectar and pollen, or the sparkle of dewdrops on the leathery leaves of kale. It is mesmerizing to watch the plants react to a soft breeze: the way the cosmos flowers wobble cheerfully above their ferny foliage, or the way the dill quivers en masse, releasing its distinct aroma in the heat of the hazy afternoon sun. It's the garden path that allows such an intimate connection, a special inside view of these little wonders that so often go unnoticed from the outside.

Paths have many practical purposes too. When it comes time to harvest, it's nice to have all the plants within easy reach. Paths offer an interesting way to break up beds and define small groupings of plants. Perhaps one of the most important things a path can do is confine footsteps to a limited area so the soil doesn't become compacted around your plants from continual stepping.

Paths can be made of stones, brick, gravel, grass, even wood chips or mulch: anything that creates a relatively clean surface to walk on. The type of path you choose goes a long way to define the style and feel of the garden, so it's important to give this some good thought before going forward. We talked about style earlier, and by this time you probably have some idea of what sort of style you prefer, whether it be formal or casual, refined or rustic. Certain materials and the way they are used lend a distinct character to the garden. For instance, imagine a highly

A path adds a sense of personality to a garden. Stone can be rustic and casual or, in this case, can be made a bit more formal by adding a brick edging. The natural texture and color of the stone grounds the garden and reflects the colors in the soil and mulch.

A soft, grass path winding its way between two garden beds lends a casual softness to this landscape filled with strawberries, dill, tomatoes, parsley, and more. Edging the path with stone or brick can help prevent grass from spreading into the garden beds.

formal knot garden. You would likely expect a very clean, distinct path made of very tightly shorn grass, evenly laid brick, or pea-gravel with edging to keep it in place. Clean, ordered, precise.

Grass, brick, and pea-gravel could also be used in a more casual design as well. A soft, curving grass path winding easily through plantings, would give something of a relaxed, cottage feel to the garden. A grass path can help to unify a yard in which most of the space has been transitioned to garden beds and only a bit left as lawn. The path creates a soft connection between the lawn areas and pulls it all together as one. If brick is laid somewhat loosely, allowing a little grass or creeping ground cover to grow up through the gaps, it would take on a more aged, rustic feel. And finally, if a pea-gravel path were bordered by rocks, or even allowed to scatter out along the edges, the feel would be more that of a country road than a formal walkway. So you see, many different materials can take on very different styles depending on how they're used, and this allows your own personal style to come through.

Your garden may not be large enough to require full-blown paths. However, even in the smallest setting, a few stepping stones offer a welcoming invitation into the heart of your garden. And that little extra step toward the plants makes picking an eggplant or a few currants much easier. In fact, stepping stones are a great addition to any garden because they give you a clean spot to step if you need to reach in a bit farther to pull a few weeds or trim a few branches.

Reclaimed brick laid loosely in a gentle curve is rustic and earthy, and gives new life to an old material. Not to mention the variety of color in the brick is reflected in the containers and plants lining the path.

A few stones nestled into the soil provide a clean place to step when harvesting a few strawberries or sage leaves. A quick and easy path can be made with just a few stones.

Wood chips or various types of mulch you find in bags at the garden center or home store can be quick, easy, and effective materials for a path through the garden. When creating a path of mulch or wood chips, it can be helpful to dig out the path a bit so it is lower than the beds around it. A couple of inches should do the trick. The soil removed from the path can be added to the garden beds. This way, when the path is filled with mulch it is contained in the channel and doesn't spill out onto the beds. Digging down a bit also allows you to fill the path with three inches or so of mulch material, which goes a long way to preventing weeds.

Whatever style and material you choose, remember the important aspects of having garden paths are to provide easy access to the plants and to prevent stepping on, and therefore compacting, the soil around the plants. Keeping footsteps confined to these paths, even if they're simply a few well-placed stones, will keep the soil around the plants light and aerated, allowing for healthy roots and happy plants.

A formal herb garden is well-served by a neatly laid brick path. When choosing path materials, keep in mind neighboring materials and textures. The deep red brick of these paths contrasts nicely with the weathered gray wood of the house and makes the greens in the herb beds pop.

A simpler path could not be found than one made of wood or bark mulch. Earthy, natural, and soft underfoot, a wood mulch path allows the colors of the plants to shine. Here a playful combination of petunias, beans, chard, and herbs show off their colors and textures on the border of the path.

VERTICAL ELEMENTS

Verticality in the garden is often overlooked. In part, I believe this is because most of us plan our gardens by imagining them from above. What I mean is, most of us draw out our garden space on paper as though we were looking at it from the sky. This is a great way to start, and certainly helps determine plant placement and spacing, but it's important to imagine your yard from eye level and think about the heights of different plants and structures. This helps ensure that tall plants and structures won't shade out or block short plants from view and also makes the landscape visually interesting.

To achieve verticality in the garden, you can simply choose some tall plants like sunflowers, artichokes, and corn. These grow anywhere from four to ten feet tall and can be stately background plants. Let's not forget all the trailing and vining plants, either. With a little structure to climb on, these plants become striking vertical features. Teepees, obelisks, arbors, trellises, pergolas, fences, or simple vine poles are easy to find, fun to build, and help set the tone of your yard, depending on the style and materials you choose.

You can purchase decorative structures to train climbing plants on, but you can also easily and inexpensively build structures that work just as well. Simple bamboo teepees are a great place to start. They're cheap, quick, and easy to assemble, and can easily be moved around the garden from year to year. An added bonus to using a teepee or other structure with plenty of space underneath: that space can be used to grow shorter plants that appreciate a bit of shade. When I plant beans or cucumbers to grow on a teepee, I plant lettuces inside the teepee. Early in the season, before the beans or cucumbers have filled in, the lettuce has plenty of sun to get established. Once the summer heat sets in, the climbing plants have filled in and provide some shade for the lettuce.

You could build a teepee or other vertical structure out of sticks and branches collected from your yard for a rustic feel or create something more formal out of painted lumber. However you go about it, a structure like this guides the plant into a pleasing form, provides air circulation to keep the plant healthy, and exposes the plant to the maximum amount of sun. And it gives your garden season-long vertical interest.

Here's a good example: An indeterminate tomato is a great plant to grow on a teepee or arbor. When we think tomatoes, we usually think of those metal cages, ladders and all the other strange contraptions invented as foolproof tomato supports. That is fine, and I'm sure they work well. But how do they look in the garden? Personally, I don't think they look so hot. Sure, once the plants are mature you never even see the structure, but what about the early

AT LEFT: Unlikely objects can make the best trellises for climbing plants. An old iron bench is a striking addition to the garden and provides the perfect support for a climbing tomato plant.

AT RIGHT: Climbing plants do wonders for bringing verticality into the garden, provided they're given something interesting to climb on. Malabar spinach wraps its vining stems tightly around any structure, making quite a statement among lower growing plants.

TOP LEFT: A simple teepee made of bamboo stakes or thin tree branches offers lots of support to vigorous climbers like cucumbers. Not only is the shape of the structure visually interesting, but the shape the plant takes on as it grows on the teepee becomes just as appealing. Plus, the cucumbers will dangle conveniently, making harvest a breeze.

TOP RIGHT: This rusted iron lattice picks up the colors in the potting bench and terra cotta pots nearby, contrasts nicely with the blue-gray color of the house, and softens a sharp corner. It also gives this indeterminate tomato the perfect place to climb.

OPPOSITE PAGE: Get creative with materials to build attractive and functional plant supports that look great in the garden. Steel reinforcing bar (a.k.a. rebar) is inexpensive, and with a welder or even a bit of wire it can be used to construct sculptural plant supports. The rusty patina is a plus too!

weeks of the season when those plants are tiny? All you see then is this monstrous metal cage in the garden. I don't relish the idea of looking at that until mid-July when my tomatoes have grown enough to cover it up. Now imagine a wrought-iron obelisk—with gracefully curved sides topped off with an iron ball—standing elegantly in your yard while young, tender plants begin filling in around it. As the season progresses, a tiny-fruited 'Red Currant' or a classic heirloom like 'Cherokee Purple' climbs its way up the obelisk, often with little or no training necessary. Imagine those dusky purple tomatoes dangling over the sturdy iron rungs of the obelisk, their color deepening with the warmth of the sun. Sounds pretty nice, doesn't it? Sure beats a flimsy tomato cage any day.

PERENNIALS

When planning a new edible landscape, I start thinking about perennials right away. Because so many vegetable plants are annuals in the northern region where I live, I like to get some perennials established to create a permanent foundation for my planting areas. It's nice to know that certain things will be back every year. I generally choose ornamental plants that have a lot of color, have a long bloom period, and are great at attracting pollinators and other beneficial insects. With these flowering perennials as a backdrop, I can fill in with annual edibles (and a few ornamental annuals for bursts of vivid color), rotating the edibles each year, and keeping the general feel of the garden the same.

The bright lavender and copper colors of purple coneflower can be relied on year after year to provide a long season of color. This year they are backing a tapestry of green plants including horseradish, sage, basil, and parsley.

By choosing a range of perennials with overlapping bloom times, you can introduce an entire season of color into your landscape and attract beneficial insects all season long. Some perennials even bring year-round structure into the garden, similar to trees and shrubs.

EDIBLE FLOWERS

A true two-for-one in the garden is the edible flower. Not only do edible flowers bring color and diversity to the garden, but you can actually harvest and eat them too. I try to work in as many edible flowers as possible to extend the "edibility" of my garden as far as I can. Many of the edible flowers are fast-growing annuals and fill in quickly.

CONTAINERS

Often thought of as the apartment-dweller's answer to gardening, containers bring unique style and flexibility to any garden of any size. They can elevate short plants to new heights or contain rascally spreading plants like mint and raspberries. Do you want to grow blueberries, but don't have acidic soil? Containers are your answer. By creating your own potting mix, you can create soil perfectly suited for acid-loving blueberries, cranberries, and their ornamental kin, rhododendrons and azaleas.

Tuck a couple of bush-type zucchini or summer squash seeds into a large container, and by midsummer you'll have an impressive plant with succulent squash resting on the edges of the container. By growing squash in a container, you can essentially double the productivity of your space. With those large plants elevated above the ground, you'll have plenty of space around the base of the container to plant chard, lettuces, other greens, herbs, annuals—whatever you choose. Remember though, if you grow a vining squash, it's going to spill right over the edges and trail along the ground just as much as if you planted it in the ground. Stick to the bush-type for containers.

I love to place containers here and there in my garden beds, for a little something unexpected. A tomato planted in a large container looks majestic climbing on a fine, ornamental trellis. The same can be said for beans or cucumbers. Imagine these surrounded by a variety of fragrant herbs and colorful annuals like verbena or petunias spilling over the edges.

Let's not forget about hanging baskets. A fine-textured, small-fruited tomato tumbling over the edges of a hanging basket is a glorious sight. Fill the extra space with annuals and herbs and you've got a basket bursting with color and flavor. It can be a fun project for kids to create theme baskets (or any other container), like a salsa basket complete

Lettuce is the perfect plant for a container: there are countless varieties of color and leaf shape, making virtually any combination striking without even adding any other plants. Pick an interesting container, like this tall, square terra cotta pot, and the result will be exquisite.

emily's 10 favorite edible flowers

· · · · · ·

Edible flowers are a delightful addition to the landscape and a treat to use in the kitchen. They offer color to salads and are bound to impress your dinner guests. My ten favorites have all the qualities of a great landscape plant, with the added bonus of being edible!

Anise hyssop

Bachelor button

Borage

Calendula

Dianthus

Monarda/bee balm

Nasturtium

Scented geranium

Signet marigold

Viola

with tomatoes, peppers, cilantro, and even some small onions or chives. Or how about a pizza basket with tomatoes and peppers, basil, oregano, parsley, and again small onions or chives? Then of course there's the salad basket bursting with lettuces, kale, a few small herbs, and, for a bit of edible color, nasturtium or calendula.

Some plants are particularly well-suited to combinations and close growing conditions. I like to mix up the plants in my containers, instead of planting a tomato in this one and a pepper in that one. Treat container edibles as you would other planters, and mix in a few ornamentals for extra color and excitement. Remember the three rules of container gardening: thrill, fill, and spill. Choose plants to fulfill each of these, and you'll have a spectacular container. The thrill is, naturally, the "wow" feature of the container—usually something tall. The fill can be a combination of plants that fill in the middle ground of the container. I usually think of greens or some other leafy plant. Then there's the spill, a trailing plant that softens the rim of the container and completes the look. Trailing herbs or annual flowers are great spillers!

ABOVE: Create a unique and striking container by focusing on texture and limiting colors, in this case to subtle greens and bronze. Shiny lime-green basil is backed by leathery kale. Stalks of millet rise above with a smooth, arching grace, and echo the color of purple basil and a few decorative ornaments.

AT RIGHT: The sweet potato vine is a mainstay in large containers where it sweeps gracefully over the edges. Even the ornamental varieties of sweet potato produce edible tubers, however the size and flavor won't match that of a true vegetable variety.

· · · · · ·

Lots of edibles do well in containers and look fantastic too! Combinations of various edibles and ornamentals make for gorgeous and handy harvests.

Blueberries

Indeterminate tomatoes

Kale

Leaf lettuces

Oregano

Parsley

Peppers

Strawberries

Swiss chard

Thyme

TOP: A simple cherry tomato in a moss basket can be the epitome of grace and delight. Who could resist plucking a few of these gorgeous gems, especially when the basket hangs right outside the kitchen door?

BOTTOM: Swiss chard is the perfect filler in this edible/ornamental combo container. The golden stems and fleshy deep green leaves set the stage for this gold and red themed combo that includes ornamental trailing petunias, snapdragons, and mandevilla climbing up a simple bamboo teepee. Sweet potato vine fills in the base with its lemon-lime foliage.

picnic on the balcony

Choose a lightweight, soilless potting mix for containers. This will give the roots air as well as moisture. You'll need fertilizer, too. Thankfully, most garden centers offer great organic fertilizers specially formulated for containers.

Single plants in containers are nice, but combinations of edibles work beautifully. Try a combo like tomato, chard, basil, calibrachoa, and oregano. This will give you tall, midlevel, and trailing plants to fill out every bit of the container.

Speaking of containers, collect a fun assortment in various sizes and shapes. Remember, just about anything with space inside can be used as a plant container. Just don't forget drainage!

CALIBRACHOA

TOMATO

CHARD

LAVENDER

ROSEMARY

OREGANO

CALIBRACHOA

PEPPER

CILANTRO

KALE

STRAWBERRY

Don't let the air go bare. Hang pots here and there with greens, strawberries and herbs, or trailing plants like tomatoes and tomatillos.

You could create a combination theme of a few plants, and repeat it in different containers, switching out a plant here and there for variety. This will give your balcony a united look.

Finally, don't forget to give your roots plenty of space. A bigger plant needs a larger pot to support it. A small pot means the plant probably won't grow to its fullest potential.

MIZUNA MUSTARD

DWARF CITRUS TREE

EGGPLANT

BASIL

ALYSSUM

LETTUCE MIX

ZUCCHINI

RAISED BEDS

Raised beds can be the answer if you have hard clay soil, if you want to elevate plants to make them easier to access, or if you want to introduce exciting new levels to your landscape. Raised beds are often used in commercial horticulture to improve drainage and to allow earlier planting (the raised soil warms up faster in spring), and the same benefits can be found in the edible landscape. The special thing about raised beds is you can squeeze a lot into a little space because of that deep, rich soil volume. For those of you who, like me, tend to over-plant a bit, this is the perfect place to do it.

These brand-new raised beds make great use of the space in a narrow, sloping, urban backyard. The beds can now be filled with high-quality soil for growing edibles and ornamentals. Mulch covers a hard gravel surface around the beds.

This limestone raised bed picks up the steel-gray colors of the house beyond and makes a perfect home for tomatoes, corn, and irises, among others.

Commonly, raised beds are built of lumber in squares or rectangles, but you don't have to stop at these shapes. Your yard may be yearning for curves made of stone or perhaps woven willow branches. Anything you can stack, pile, or otherwise make into a short wall can be used to form raised beds. (Avoid using treated wood or any other materials that could leach contaminants into the soil.) Fill your beds with good-quality soil, peat, and compost, and you've got a perfect spot for growing a beautiful and delicious garden. Keep in mind, since raised beds are so well-drained, they'll also tend to dry out a little faster than the ground around them. A thick layer of mulch will help hold some of that moisture a bit longer, but you may have to water a little more often than you would if you planted directly in the ground.

Raised beds can be used to set aside space for plants with special growing considerations. A simple stone bed filled with an acidic peat mixture makes a perfect place for growing acid-loving blueberries. Beyond the blueberries, squash grows in the garden soil below.

annual raised beds

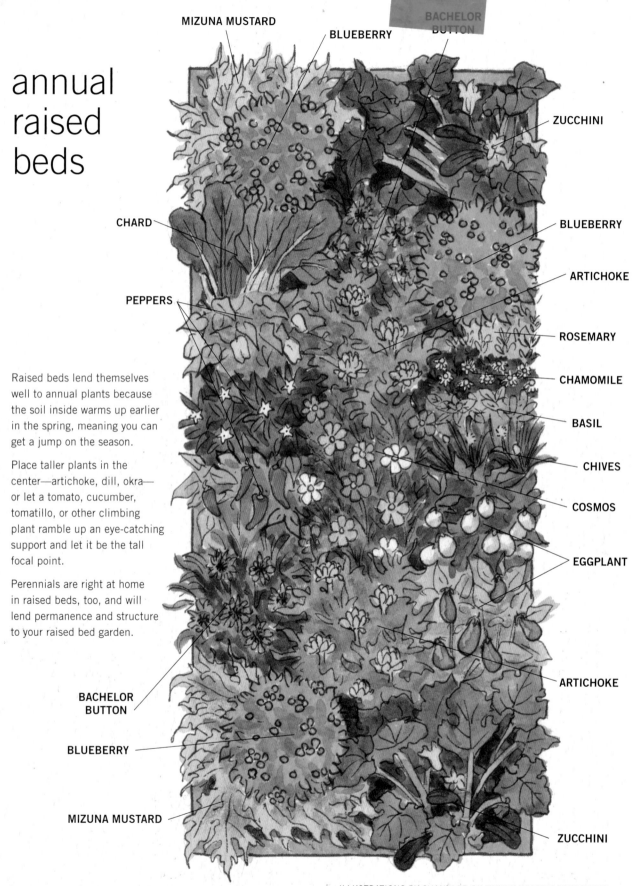

MIZUNA MUSTARD

BLUEBERRY

ZUCCHINI

CHARD

BLUEBERRY

ARTICHOKE

ROSEMARY

PEPPERS

CHAMOMILE

BASIL

Raised beds lend themselves well to annual plants because the soil inside warms up earlier in the spring, meaning you can get a jump on the season.

Place taller plants in the center—artichoke, dill, okra— or let a tomato, cucumber, tomatillo, or other climbing plant ramble up an eye-catching support and let it be the tall focal point.

Perennials are right at home in raised beds, too, and will lend permanence and structure to your raised bed garden.

CHIVES

COSMOS

EGGPLANT

ARTICHOKE

BACHELOR BUTTON

BLUEBERRY

MIZUNA MUSTARD

ZUCCHINI

ILLUSTRATIONS BY CHANDLER O'LEARY (ANAGRAM-PRESS.COM)

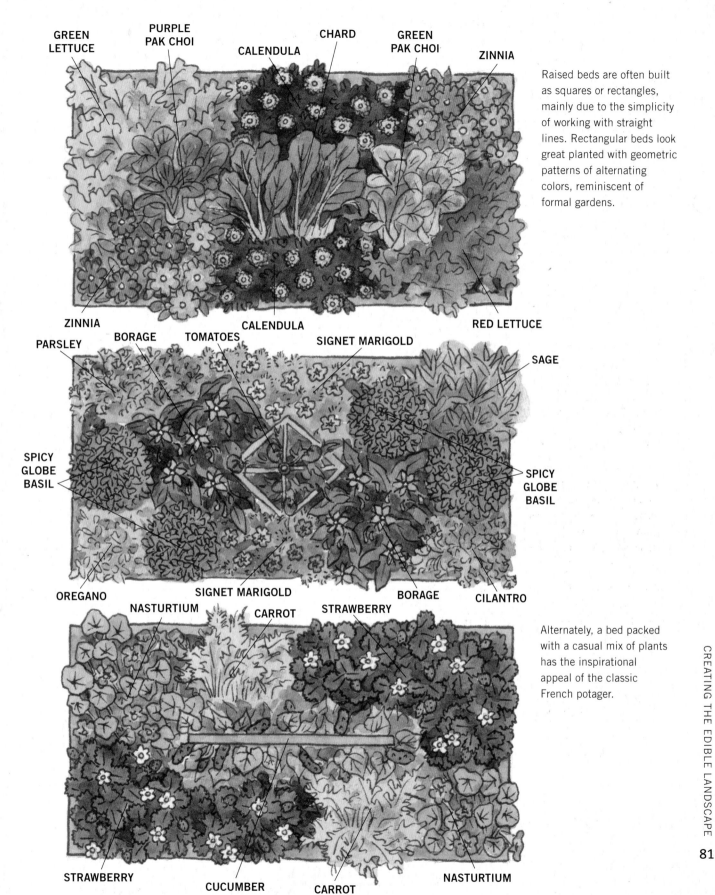

GREEN LETTUCE

PURPLE PAK CHOI

CALENDULA

CHARD

GREEN PAK CHOI

ZINNIA

Raised beds are often built as squares or rectangles, mainly due to the simplicity of working with straight lines. Rectangular beds look great planted with geometric patterns of alternating colors, reminiscent of formal gardens.

ZINNIA

CALENDULA

RED LETTUCE

PARSLEY

BORAGE

TOMATOES

SIGNET MARIGOLD

SAGE

SPICY GLOBE BASIL

SPICY GLOBE BASIL

OREGANO

SIGNET MARIGOLD

BORAGE

CILANTRO

NASTURTIUM

CARROT

STRAWBERRY

Alternately, a bed packed with a casual mix of plants has the inspirational appeal of the classic French potager.

STRAWBERRY

CUCUMBER

CARROT

NASTURTIUM

season of
plenty

We've been talking a lot about creativity, design, texture, color, form—rather intangible concepts. I imagine you're ready for some real, nitty-gritty, let's-get-our-fingers-dirty conversation. Well, you've reached the place in the book where we talk seeds, water, insects, diseases, wildlife, harvesting, and all that good stuff. This is where we start to see things grow and take steps to keep it all healthy, productive, and looking spectacular.

In containers, in raised beds, or in the ground, edibles and ornamentals can be planted anywhere and in any combination as long as they have good-quality soil, water, and plenty of light. This rustic brick patio is bursting with container-grown tomatoes, eggplant, peppers, greens, and herbs. The raised bed holds more herbs and flowers, and even provides a place to sit. Beyond the patio, this densely planted yard boasts apple trees, raspberries, strawberries, and rhubarb.

There are little things you can do from the very start and all throughout the season to make your landscape more productive, more attractive, and more fun (meaning easier). By keeping these in mind throughout the season, the garden can be a delightful place of beauty and bounty.

IT ALL STARTS WITH A SEED

One of the best things about starting your own seeds is the unbelievably vast array of choices you have. Rather than having to choose from the limited selection of transplants at the garden center, you have a world of options at hand. The garden centers generally choose reliable, popular, high-quality varieties to grow and sell. If that is your only option, you're bound to get some good plants. But, if you're looking for unique varieties, unusual colors, and textures, you're going to want to start your own seeds.

Thankfully, most vegetables grow quite easily from seed. Greens grow very quickly and often do best if you sow the seeds right in the ground where you intend for them to grow. It's easier and faster to thin greens seedlings in the garden than it is to transplant the tiny, tender seedlings from flats to the garden.

Chard is an easy plant to start from seed. Even the tiny seedlings have vibrant colored stems, so if you've planted a color mix, you'll know early in the season what you've got.

Warm-season crops like tomatoes, eggplant, zucchini, and others that have long germination-to-maturity times are best started indoors a few weeks before the last frost date. That way you'll get a jump on the season, your plants will fill in faster, they'll produce food sooner, and everything will look better for a longer time. Take a look at the back of a seed packet and you'll see something there about the number of days to maturity. It generally goes like this: for plants that are usually direct-seeded in the garden, the days to maturity means the number of days from sowing the seed to harvest; for plants that are usually put in the garden as transplants, the days to maturity is the number of days from transplanting outdoors to harvest. I'm not sure why they can't be consistent, but they're not, so keep that in mind when you're scheduling seeds. Keep in mind also, that those numbers are based on ideal growing conditions, something that most of us are not so fortunate to have.

If you want some good suggestions about when to start certain seeds and when to plant them out, I find the best info comes from local university extension websites. Most offer charts for planting times that are based on actual experience and trials in the local climate by people who understand plants. University resources often explain things better than commercial websites and seed companies, because they are written for the home-grower audience and reference region-specific conditions and climate concerns.

INTO THE GROUND

Planting is such an exciting time, because the garden starts to take shape and you begin to see your plans and ideas come to life. One of the most important things to remember when transplanting your plants is to be sure the weather and soil are warm enough. Plants started indoors should be given some time to harden off, which involves setting them outdoors to get used to the new environment, but doing so gradually in a spot that is protected from harsh conditions like wind, rain, intense sun, and cold. I've found it best to set plants out for a few hours a day at first, gradually increasing the time until the plants are well-adjusted. I've made the mistake of taking plants directly from indoors into the ground, and they repaid me by looking very weak and stressed and growing very slowly.

There's no need to buy expensive materials if you want to start seeds at home. Virtually any container can be used to start seeds, like plastic cups with a few holes poked in the bottom for drainage.

CHAPTER FOUR

starting seeds

You don't need a greenhouse or fancy, expensive equipment to start your own seeds. You don't even need to buy plastic trays, cell-packs, or fiber pots made specifically for the purpose. Inexpensive plastic cups or used yogurt containers work just as well for starting seeds. Poke a few small holes in the bottoms of the cups for drainage and keep them in a tray to protect the surface they're sitting on. Generally, it works best to sow one seed per container. This will eliminate having to thin the plants and prevents competition. Sowing a lot of seeds in a large container will cause headaches down the road when it's time to transplant, because all the roots will grow together and be difficult to separate. Pulling apart the roots at transplanting time can also damage the plants. Best to keep one seed in a small container.

The one thing I suggest you spring for is a good seed-starting mix. What makes seed-starting mixes different from typical potting mixes is they generally have finer texture so the seed is sure to have better contact with the mix, and the light texture allows the roots to develop easily. Many seed-starting mixes have little or no nutrients. This is okay for seed germination, but once the plants emerge and put on a few leaves they'll need nutrients. A diluted fertilizer solution can be used once a week to supply the nutrients the plants need to develop.

You want the plants you start from seed to be vigorous and healthy, so you'll need to be sure they have the right environment for optimal growth. Basically, they need consistently warm temperatures, a lot of light, and consistent moisture. Find a spot in your house that stays warm and is away from drafts. Provide adequate light to keep the seedlings from becoming spindly or "leggy." Natural light inside a house is generally not enough. Inexpensive fluorescent tube light fixtures work well for starting seedlings indoors. A timer can be set to give the plants the appropriate amount of light, generally between twelve and sixteen hours per day. Finally, consistent moisture is very important. The small volume of growing mix can dry out quickly, and a tiny seedling doesn't have much in the way of moisture reserves. A spray bottle is a gentle way to provide water to delicate seeds and seedlings.

You can go from very simple to very complex when in comes to starting seeds indoors: a few trays under a fluorescent light in the kitchen to a structure of shelves with integrated lighting, heat mats, and so on. You don't need all that to be successful, especially if you're only starting a few seeds for a small garden. My advice, as with most things, is to start small. Pick a few plants you want to start from seed and give it a try. If you enjoy the process and you have the space, then you can build up from there.

Check out the Resources section in the back of this book for more detail on starting seeds. Check your local resources for advice on seeding dates.

Direct-seeded plants can usually be sown shortly after the soil has thawed in the spring. Depending on your climate, it might be advisable to wait a little longer, as the tender seedlings that emerge will be very delicate and could be easily damaged by a late-spring frost.

When it comes to spacing plants in the garden, I err on the side of too close. In my experience, it seems I've had fewer weeds when my plants are placed close together, because the healthy and vigorous plants shade and out-compete the weed

Spacing is an important consideration, especially for plants like these heading lettuces. Not only must they have the proper space to grow, you will better be able to enjoy the beautiful form of the plant as it grows in the garden. The violas and parsley were spaced closer with the intention of them growing close and intermingling.

seedlings. This is a delicate balance however, because the denser the plants, the more competition and the better the conditions are for disease. But I enjoy the look of a dense garden, so I take the risk. Occasionally throughout the season I have to remove plants when things get a little too dense, and the remaining plants fill the gaps quickly and naturally.

If your style errs on the side of more space, it will likely be easier to access all the plants without harming others in the process. You'll also prevent a lot of diseases from cropping up by giving the plants plenty of airflow and light. In general, the seed packs and garden centers know best when they advise certain spacing. It's easy to forget that the plants are going to get a lot bigger than they are at planting time, and it's important to figure that into your spacing. Sure, the garden may be a little sparse for a couple of weeks but your plants will likely be healthier and more productive in the long run.

THINNING, PINCHING, AND PRUNING

Throughout the season, many plants respond well to a little primping. Through thinning, pinching, and pruning, you will give your plants more room to grow, help promote branching and fullness, and prevent unwanted spread.

Thinning is a task generally reserved for the areas of the garden where seeds are sown directly into the ground. Lettuce, kale, carrots, radishes, even calendula, are plants I regularly thin a few weeks after seeding. Many direct-sown seeds are so small it's almost impossible to avoid placing two or three . . . or ten into one hole. Attempting to remove a minuscule carrot seed after it's in the ground is not worth the effort, but thinning the seedlings after a couple of weeks certainly is.

Thinning is important so the plants have adequate room to grow. Take carrots, for example. If carrots are sown the way I described above, you may end up with five carrots trying to grow in the same spot. This will result in one of two things: 1) none of the carrots will grow very large because they're competing for the space, or 2) the carrots will be gnarled and twisted as they try to find their own little spot of soil in which to grow. By thinning the plants to one every inch or two, each plant will have adequate space to grow a large, straight root. The concept also applies to plants whose above-ground parts we use. Lettuces are easy to sow far too close together, and when they start to grow, they become a mass of leaves too cramped to grow very large. When they're small seedlings, plucking out the smaller, weaker-looking plants will leave room for the vigorous ones to grow into lush and tender greens. Thinning lettuces is one of my favorite tasks, because the diminutive, tender seedlings go right into my salad bowl for an early-season treat.

Pinching is a well-known tactic in the ornamental garden as a way to promote branching and more blooms. By pinching off the main growing tip (and dead-heading spent blooms) right above a lower set of leaves, growth will be diverted from the main stem and new side shoots will grow and produce a more compact, bushy plant often with more blooms. This can also be done early in the season to help promote vigorous root growth. Commonly, annual flowers grown in a greenhouse are encouraged to flower early so they look good to shoppers. However, all the plant's energy is being put into those flowers, so when you get the plant home and put it in the ground, chances are it's not going to develop a very vigorous root system. The same can be said for many perennials, vegetables, and fruits. Removing early-season flowers can help promote stronger plants and better fruiting later on. If these plants produce flowers very early in the season, they won't be putting their energy into strong roots, and the plant may never flourish. Though it's a tough thing to do, I make myself pinch back the first wave of flowers on many plants when I first set them out in the garden. It seems counterintuitive, but the plants generally end up being more vigorous and productive in the long run.

For some plants, we want to prevent flowering as long as possible. Take basil, for example. It's generally understood that basil loses its sweet flavor once it flowers. Therefore, all season long, any time I'm in the garden, I pinch off the tops of my basil. This promotes side branching, which means more tasty leaves, and delays flowering. The same can be said for many other herbs. Harvest continually by pinching, and flowering will be delayed.

TOP: These tender young lettuce seedlings will need to be thinned to have adequate space to grow. By gently tugging at the base of the seedling, pull out enough plants to leave an inch or more space between those remaining. Don't throw them away though. Trim off the roots and wash the leaves before tossing into a salad.
AUTHOR PHOTO

BOTTOM: These mustard green seedlings have been thinned to about fifteen inches apart so they'll have room to grow to their full size without getting too crowded.

Tomatoes are a little different story, and I hesitate even to bring up the issue here since people's opinions vary so much on whether or not to pinch tomatoes. Some say absolutely not, let them do their natural thing. Some say pinch and even prune them severely to direct energy into the developing tomatoes and not into further vegetative growth. I've tried a combination of all of those to varying degrees of success. I highly recommend pinching off side shoots (suckers), mainly because the plants become unruly if all those are allowed to grow unchecked. The plant ends up bushy, dense, hard to control, and prone to disease due to poor air circulation. Additionally, the plant will produce more tomatoes than I can find within all that vegetation, and they will likely be small. This is most important for the indeterminate types that will grow like crazy and produce more tomatoes than the plant can support. The determinate types don't typically need it, but I tend to do it anyway because I don't mind sacrificing a few tomatoes for a better-looking plant. The best way to find out if a plant responds well to pinching is to try it yourself. You can certainly read a lot of advice about which plants to pinch and how to do it, and that's a good place to start. But you'll never know how it works until you try it yourself and keep track of what happens.

While the flowers on this sweet basil look lovely, their presence means the flavor of the basil will likely decline. Keep the flavors of basil, mint, and other herbs at their peak by pinching back the growing tips regularly before flowers initiate. Simply pinch off the stem below the top set of leaves, just above the next set.

Pruning is a bit more aggressive than pinching and can be performed on herbaceous plants as well as woody shrubs and trees. While pruning of fruit trees and shrubs is generally kept to the dormant season, some plants can tolerate minor pruning in the growing season to control growth or especially to remove dead or diseased plant parts. Some vining plants like squash and cucumber can be pruned to control their growth, removing the growing tip or even entire vine laterals. But remember, any pruning done in the middle of the season makes a plant particularly susceptible to diseases because of the open wounds. So prune carefully.

WATER AND IRRIGATION

Water is the lifeblood of the garden, and unfortunately rain does not always come consistently enough to keep a garden adequately watered. Irrigation of lawns and gardens is a touchy subject in many areas, as water resources are becoming more and more limited. I always feel a bit more justified using water to irrigate a garden that includes food plants, since the water is in essence being used to feed people. That justification might be considered a stretch and doesn't always suffice when there are water restrictions set in place.

Thankfully, there are responsible ways to water a garden to get the very most out of this valuable resource. I've had the best experience with drip irrigation, which directs the water right into the soil and to the plants' roots where it is needed most, reducing wasted water from overspray and evaporation. Specialized hoses with drip ports or soaker hoses work best when run underneath mulch, which makes the system even better because that well-directed water is held in the ground by the mulch and the mulch hides the hoses, keeping the garden looking clean and tidy. (Mulch can sometimes clog the drip ports depending on the type of drip system used and the type of mulch covering it.) It may cost a little money and take a bit of time to get the system set up, but the benefits of this type of irrigation make it worthwhile.

Another advantage of drip irrigation is that it can help prevent disease in the garden. Many disease pathogens require water to move around and thrive in humid conditions. By minimizing the amount of water on the leaves of the plants (limiting it to rain), pathogen movement is limited, the canopy of plants remains drier, and disease incidence may be reduced.

Micro-drip systems are available for container gardens too, which is a great help for the busy gardener. Container plants tend to dry out very quickly, and if you forget to water for

A micro-drip system can be used to keep your container gardens lush all season. This type of system works well in a small garden bed too.

a few days it's difficult to rejuvenate the wilted plants. By setting up a system of drip heads in each of your containers, and connecting it to a water source with a timer, your plants will be watered regularly even if you're out of town.

If you use a traditional sprinkler, be sure to give some thought as to where you place it so as not to waste the water on sidewalks, patios, and other areas where the water will simply wash away or evaporate. Perhaps set the water on a lower pressure and water smaller areas at a time with a low spray so the water is directed more toward the ground than into the sky. Experiment to find the best type of sprinkler for your space and the best way to use water wisely.

Go the extra step to conserving water and install rain barrels around your house. While at one time these barrels were unsightly and cumbersome, more decorative versions are available that look more sculptural than utilitarian. Rain barrels can be found made of plastic, wood, and terra cotta; they are available in all shapes and sizes from traditional casks to graceful urns. I've even seen rain barrels that impersonate boulders and many that include a planter at the top to grow colorful annuals, cheery strawberries, herbs, or whatever you like. Yet another reminder not to stop at the obvious, but to be creative and seek out garden elements that will enhance your space visually as well as practically.

A traditional overhead sprinkler may not be as efficient as a drip system, but will certainly do the trick. Find the style that works best for your space and directs water to the plants without over-spraying onto impermeable surfaces such as sidewalks and driveways.

MULCH

I always think my garden is looking pretty good in late spring when the transplants are all in the ground, and the plants I've direct-seeded start to fill in. But then I add a layer of mulch and I am amazed at how much better it all looks. Suddenly there's uniformity to the garden that wasn't there before: the deep, dark color of the mulch unifying all the different areas of the garden. The mulch is like a dark canvas from which the color of the plants seems to explode. It's that visual contrast I love most about using mulch in the garden. Of course there are many more practical benefits, but it surely doesn't hurt that mulch looks so good.

Water management can be a finicky thing in the midst of a hot summer, and mulch steps right up to help out. With a couple of inches of mulch over the soil, water will trickle gently down through the mulch into the soil and be more available to roots because of this slow movement. Once the moisture is in the soil, mulch helps retain that moisture by slowing evaporation, making that water available to plants for a longer time and reducing the amount of water you'll have to provide. A hilly garden sometimes has the added challenge of erosion, as water tends to wash away the soil. A layer of mulch will help prevent soil loss, again, by slowing water movement.

Mulch also acts as insulation for the soil, keeping it cooler on hot days and warmer on chilly days. This insulating effect prevents drastic temperature changes that can be stressful to plants.

Depending on the type you use, mulch can also add valuable nutrients to the soil. Generally these are provided in small amounts, but with continued use over time the mulch is a good source of slow-release nutrients. Also dependent upon the type of mulch is its ability to improve soil structure. Organic mulches like compost and well-rotted manure are the most effective at both providing nutrients and improving soil structure. The organic material in the mulch stimulates microbial activity. As these organisms break down the organic matter, nutrients are released into the soil, the soil is aerated and the organic matter aids in the water-holding capacity of the soil.

Yet another of my favorite virtues of mulch is its ability to keep plants, flowers, fruits, and vegetables clean. Because mulch prevents a lot of splashing of water, less debris will splash up onto the plants. Also, the top layer of the mulch tends to dry quickly, so strawberries or other fruits resting on mulch may be cleaner, drier and less prone to disease.

Having extolled some of the virtues of mulch, I should mention the various types. My favorite mulch to use is aged compost. Compost mulch is dark and rich, contains variously sized particles so it has a somewhat coarse texture, and is relatively dense so it creates a solid cover to prevent weed growth. Throughout the season, as the compost decomposes further, it adds nutrients to the soil.

As far as appearance goes, shredded bark and wood chips are second in my opinion but there's a catch. These materials break down very slowly. If used in beds that are replanted each year, you'll be attempting to dig through chunks of wood, which can be frustrating. Also, as the wood slowly breaks down it actually takes nitrogen from the soil for that process. Once broken down, the nitrogen will be returned to the soil, but it can take years for wood chip mulch to break down completely. A layer on top of the soil can perform very nicely to retain moisture, moderate soil temperature, and prevent weed seed

Compost mulch creates a dark carpet under and around plants, making their colors pop. Spread two inches or so around plants after they've become well-established. The compost will continue to decompose throughout the season, contributing valuable nutrients to the soil.

Shredded wood and wood chips have a very natural look when used as mulch and work well to slow water movement, retain moisture, and moderate soil temperature. They're difficult to dig through, so be sure to clear the mulch away before digging or planting late-season plants.

germination, but you might want to rake it away before planting next season so it doesn't get incorporated into the soil.

Hulls of rice, cacao, pecan, peanut, and so on are available in some areas and look attractive in the garden. The lighter hulls have a tendency to blow away in the wind, but the heavier ones stay in place nicely. I like the dark brown color of cacao hulls, but they have sharp edges and can make working in the garden a little uncomfortable. An added warning on cacao hulls: they are known to be harmful to pets if consumed (as chocolate is).

Pine needles (or pine straw) make a fine-textured, attractive mulch that is resistant to compaction. Pine mulch is acidic and can be beneficial when used around acid-loving plants. Its acidifying effects are generally mild, therefore it can be used around most garden plants.

Artificial materials commonly used as mulches include landscape fabric and plastic. I generally shy away from these, primarily because of appearance and the challenge of working with them. These have to be laid before planting, and the plants inserted through the mulch. This makes direct seeding a challenge, and requires a lot of pre-planning for transplants. These two materials are very effective at preventing weed growth, so if that is a major concern in your garden it may be worth trying them. A natural mulch can be applied over the top to improve the appearance. While landscape fabric allows for movement of water, plastic of course is impermeable. If using plastic mulch, be sure to run drip irrigation underneath it.

A tidy, weed-free garden means more room for all your luscious edibles to grow. Clear weeds away before planting in the spring and keep up with it through the season to help keep plants vigorous and cut down on insect pest and disease problems.
M. CORNELIUS/SHUTTERSTOCK

WEEDS

William Shakespeare wrote, "Small herbs have grace; great weeds grow apace." And how right he was, for it seems that in the time it takes the gardener to turn around new weeds have sprung up where moments ago there were none. This, alas, is the nature of weeds; and if one gardens, one must pull weeds.

But why? If weeds are plants, and we want a wide variety of plants in the landscape, why bother removing the weeds? For one, weeds are usually not very nice looking. They're often scraggly, spiny, or plain, growing in unrefined clumps or spreading haphazardly. However, this is not always the case, as there are many plants that were once grown as ornamentals but naturalized so easily they got out of control and became known as weeds. (You've probably heard of purple loosestrife.) It is their ability to naturalize (meaning the plant can reproduce and maintain itself without our help) and the speed at which they grow and reproduce that makes them invasive and, in turn, a problem in our gardens.

These plants compete for resources in the garden, which is one of the primary reasons they need to be controlled. Weeds need water, light, and nutrients like all plants, and their presence in the garden can result in slowed growth, decreased vigor, poor productivity, and a weaker overall appearance of desirable plants.

Weeds also harbor insects, disease pathogens, and animals that can cause a host of problems in the garden. (Yes, weeds can also provide habitat for beneficial insects, but you'll have so much variety and good-insect-attracting plants in your garden that you do not need the weeds to help attract beneficials.) Whether in the garden or along the perimeter, dense stands of weeds provide cover for these pests until the time is right for them to attack your plants.

The key to keeping weeds in check is to get to them early, especially before they go to seed. Most weeds produce a staggeringly high number of seeds per flower, and the seeds tend to germinate easily. Once those seeds are released, you will have a much larger problem to deal with. Pull or dig weeds early and regularly to keep them from self-seeding.

Many weeds spread through underground stems called rhizomes. These are particularly tricky to control because if one little section of the rhizome breaks off it can grow into a new plant. Quackgrass and Canada thistle fall into this category. These types need to be carefully dug, preferably when the soil is moist, to eliminate as much root and rhizome as possible.

Then there are those unrelenting taproot weeds that grow back again and again no matter how many times you pull them—think dandelion and dock. The deeply growing taproots on weeds like these need to be completely removed, which isn't always easy. Most often when I'm pulling these tenacious invaders, I hear the disappointing snap of the root breaking off, and I know I'll be seeing this weed again soon. Best to dig these up to get that entire root out of the ground.

Some weeds can be prevented by applying a two- to three-inch layer of mulch in the garden. Provided the mulch does not have weed seeds in it, the mulch can prevent the germination of seeds. Mulch won't take care of those persistent perennial weeds for long though, and you'll be back out there pulling those in no time. Best to try to eliminate the perennial weeds early on, before you plant the year's annual vegetables and flowers. As mentioned above, landscape fabric and plastic mulches can be very effective at preventing weed growth, but irrigation and appearance should be taken into account.

If you have a garden of any kind, you will most likely be contending with weeds. They can be a lot of work, but it's valuable work. Weeding gets you into the garden, meaning you have an opportunity to check things out, look for fruit or veggies to harvest, inspect for pests, or enjoy being out there in the midst of your plants. Or, it can mean fun time in the garden teaching your children how to identify plants, which ones are good and bad, and why they are considered so. It's all in how you look at it.

CREATURES IN THE GARDEN

We're not the only creatures on this planet that enjoy fruits and vegetables; insects, mammals, and microbes all like to feast on some of the very foods we enjoy most. To attempt to keep all creatures out of the garden would not only be futile but also a mistake, because many of those creatures are very beneficial to the success of the garden.

A balanced, healthy garden filled with a wide variety of plant families is a good start to keeping problem organisms at bay. By spending time in your garden and being aware of changes, you will likely notice if something is wrong and most likely be able to track down the source of the problem. Each area of the country has some pests that cause more trouble than others, so you'll want to be aware of local issues and be on the lookout.

Insects: The Bad Guys

There are a lot of insects in this world, and some of them are here to wreak havoc on your plants. Well, okay, it only seems as though that is their sole purpose. Their purpose on this planet is much more complex than our annoyance with them in our gardens, but sometimes it's hard to see beyond that. It's important to remember that even in our gardens, they are only doing what they naturally must do to survive, and in large part that means eating and procreating. Often on the scale of a home garden, insect pests don't cause too much of a problem. But if you have a garden for long enough, you will eventually be challenged by a few pest insects. Some years are worse than others, like some insects are worse than others.

A telltale sign of insect damage is the presence of holes: holes in the leaves, stems, and fruit. The holes might be tiny like those caused by flea beetles or large like those left behind by Japanese beetles. Insects might also cause distorted or speckled leaves, often the result of aphids or spider mites. (These symptoms, however, may also signal a disease in the plant.) When you notice signs of damage, the first thing to do is look for the cause. If you see a damaged leaf, turn it over and take a look at the underside. Insects often hide out and feed from the undersides of leaves or might be seen on the stems. Once you find an insect, stop and watch it for a while. You may see it actively eating your plant. First you should learn what the insect is, to be sure it is the one causing the damage. (This is especially important if you did not see it actually eating your plant, because many insects are not harmful to plants.) Once you know what the insect is, you can then decide how to manage the problem.

There are various levels of remedies to address insect pest problems in the garden. Large pests like tomato hornworms and Japanese beetles can simply be plucked off the plants and dropped into soapy water. Spider mites and aphids can often be dislodged and

washed away from the plants by a strong blast of water from the hose. A few treatments over a couple of weeks and that should take care of them.

There are some relatively safe treatments on the market like horticultural oils and insecticidal soaps that can be effective at controlling some pest insects. Yet, the problem with these is that while they kill the pests they also kill the beneficial insects in the garden. Therefore, I find it best to avoid using these products.

Prevention is absolutely the best way to reduce insect pests in the garden. By keeping the garden clean and clearing out any and all dead plant material during and after the season, habitat for various stages of insect pest life cycles will be greatly reduced. Eliminating weeds has the same advantage. Keeping plants healthy and vigorous by providing adequate water and nutrients helps the plants survive attacks with minimal long-lasting effects. Finally, planting a wide range of plant species will reduce large masses of host crops and keep many insects from setting up shop in your garden. All these plants will also help to attract beneficial insects, which are our best allies against pest insects.

Flea beetles have been feeding on this baby pak choi plant. Plants that have reached the four- to five-leaf stage are usually vigorous enough to handle the damage. New leaves emerging from the center have little or no damage. Flea beetles generally don't last much beyond the first few warm weeks, and the plants will outgrow the damage. AUTHOR PHOTO

emily's 10 favorite
plants for attracting beneficial insects

There are a great many plants out there that are very good at attracting beneficial insects, and some perhaps more so than those listed here. The great thing about these ten plants is that they have brought countless bees, butterflies, parasitic wasps, syrphid flies, and myriad other beneficial insects to my gardens and have looked spectacular while doing it!

Alyssum (not edible)

Bachelor button

Borage

Cosmos (not edible)

Dill

Echinacea

Fennel

Monarda/bee balm

Rudbeckia (not edible)

Yarrow (not edible)

TOP RIGHT: Lady beetles feed during their larval and adult stages on aphids, mites, and scale insects among others. Provide a welcoming habitat for the beneficial lady beetle by planting alyssum, dill, and other small-flowered plants. PALTO/SHUTTERSTOCK

Insects: The Good Guys

Chances are you'll see far more beneficial insects in the garden than pest insects. For this very reason, it is critical that when you discover an insect or a collection of eggs on a plant, you do not react by immediately smashing it, assuming it is a pest. If you're not familiar with the insect already, take some time to look it up on one of the many websites or books devoted to the subject. You may find that the insect at hand is a garden ally—a beneficial insect that provides the service of pollination or pest control.

As many pest insects as there are in the garden, there are as many, if not more, beneficial insects that prey on these pests for food. Many flies, wasps, beetles, bugs, and spiders feed on pest insects, and some even feed on weed seeds. Whether in their larval stage or adult stage, a huge variety of insects eat the eggs, larva, and adult stages of many pests.

Aside from predation of pests, many insects are key to pollination in the garden. In fact, many of the same insects that control pests in the garden also provide pollination. Some, however, specialize in pollination, the most notable of these being bees. Not only classic honeybees provide this service; many native bees, flies, and wasps do as well.

TOP LEFT: Syrphid flies, or hover flies, are tiny garden visitors who do a world of good. The larvae of many species prey on aphids, while the adults are excellent pollinators.
SHENK1/SHUTTERSTOCK

BOTTOM LEFT: The most famous beneficial insect in the garden must be the bee. They are delightful to watch as they hover from flower to flower, collecting pollen and efficiently transferring it from one flower to the next, ensuring delicious fruits and vegetables for gardeners. AUTHOR PHOTO

TOP RIGHT: Daddy longlegs, or harvestmen, may snack lightly on some plants in the garden, but are also carnivorous and feed on various soft-bodied insects including aphids, mites, caterpillars, and even small slugs. JOSEPH SCOTT PHOTOGRAPHY/SHUTTERSTOCK

BOTTOM RIGHT: The delicate flowers of chives seem irresistible to bees. These fragrant blooms attract a wide array of pollinators; however, it's a good idea to cut the flowers just before they go to seed since chives self-seed readily. HRASKA/SHUTTERSTOCK

Certain insects are better at pollinating some plants than others. Bumble bees, for instance are very efficient at pollinating blueberry flowers.

Other insects may prefer large flowers, small flowers, or other specific flower types depending on their body structure. To maintain a healthy and productive garden, we should invite as many pollinators as possible, which means planting a wide variety of plants. That is one of the great benefits of the style of gardening we're talking about here. By planting a wide range of edibles and ornamentals from many different plant families, we're creating habitat for a diverse population of insects. This means a healthy environment for our plants, and a beautiful and productive garden for us.

Mammals and Birds

While mammals are some of the easiest garden pests to see, they can be the most difficult to control. Mice, voles, squirrels, rabbits, groundhogs, gophers, deer, even moose and bears cause heartache to many a gardener. When it comes to dealing with these creatures in the garden, prevention is the best measure. Once they've taken up residence, damage is fast and furious, and eradicating them is usually a challenge.

The first step in keeping small mammals at bay is to keep a clean and tidy garden. Debris and weeds provide good cover for small animals. EDUARD KYSLYNSKYY/ SHUTTERSTOCK

The smaller of these creatures might dig up newly planted seeds, chew tiny seedlings, or even feed on mature plants throughout the garden. Damage can usually be discerned from that of insects by the larger scale and that the plants are eaten roughly from the edges as opposed to insect damage, which often creates holes in the centers of leaves. They may also burrow into the ground to feed on roots, bulbs, and tubers, causing mysterious decline of plants.

To keep these critters at bay, a good first step is to keep a clean and tidy garden. Debris and weeds provide good cover for small animals, as does grass, so keeping a good distance between grass and your garden plants might help. Woodpiles are a haven for small rodents, so it's a good idea to keep wood and other yard debris piles far from your plants. Mulch, unfortunately, is also good cover for smaller creatures, especially when it is thick and light. If rodents are a problem for you, it might help to keep your mulch cover thin—about an inch.

The larger creatures have the ability to cause an incredibly large amount of damage in an incredibly short amount of time. There are many plants that are reported to be resistant to animal pests like deer and moose, but what I've heard from gardeners who battle with these creatures is that they'll walk right past or right over those "deterrent" plants to get to the good stuff. I've also heard from countless gardeners that repellent sprays and various tricks may work for a while, but rarely offer much protection in the long run. Unfortunately, the only real way to keep large animals out of your plants is a very big fence. I know that doesn't do much for the idea of a landscape, but if you want to grow food plants in an area where large animals are present, it may be your only choice. You can, however, be creative with your fencing options and make the fence a feature.

Pets and people can be destructive to the garden too. Pets can generally be trained to keep out of the garden or even keep to paths and stepping stones. People sometimes need similar training. Some tender, young plants may need temporary protection from the wayward foot or untrained weeding hand until they are recognizable as a valuable plant. Once the plant has reached a certain size and sturdiness, the protection can be removed.

TOP: Pets can generally be trained to keep out of the garden, or even keep to paths and stepping stones. TAMI FRED/ SHUTTERSTOCK

BOTTOM: Some seedlings need protection from the wayward foot or unknowing weeding hand. Don't stop at chicken wire though. Be creative to keep the garden visually interesting. Old gas stove burners wired together become a sculptural element while protecting this tiny sage seedling.

fences as features

For some gardens, a fence may be a necessity to keep large animals or other intruders at bay. Traditionally when we think of a garden fence, we think of deer fencing, chicken wire, or some other uninspired material hastily fastened to wooden or metal posts. The appearance of the finished product is often raw and cage-like: yet another reason the proverbial vegetable garden has often been relegated to the unseen corners of the yard. But it does not have to be this way. A fence can be a lovely structure, eye-catching and inspired, adding visual interest to the garden as well as protection.

This fence might be made of crisp white pickets, reclaimed barn wood, vintage wrought iron, modern steel and polished mahogany, rustic bamboo, or willow: any material that speaks to you and fits with the overall theme of your house and yard. Yes, this fence might be tall, but it doesn't need to be oppressive. Gaps in the planks, lattice-work near the top, scalloped edges, a mixture of various materials to break up the texture, all these help to give a fence a sense of lightness and make it an intriguing addition to the yard.

What lies inside the fence can be the garden of your dreams. All the concepts that apply to creating a garden design in a fully open yard can apply inside your fenced garden. Inside your garden oasis you can play with line and form, balance and symmetry, texture, color, size, form. Just because the garden is inside a

Espaliered apple trees line this weathered fence. The pale color of the fence and the vertical slats are a sharp contrast to the tree, accentuating the shape of the trained branches and the deep green leaves for a stunning effect.

fence doesn't mean is has to be a traditional garden of rows and rows. Any style you choose will work as well inside the fence: formal, casual, or anywhere in between. And the fence itself becomes a backdrop, a canvas of sorts, from which to build up your garden of fruit and flowers, vegetables and herbs. The color and texture of the fence will set off the colors and textures of the plants—a feature not attainable in an open garden—giving you an extra level of design

to experiment with. The fence also offers structure for training plants. Espaliered fruit trees might line the fence walls; grapes, cucumbers, kiwi, hops, and countless other vining plants could ramble along the fence, providing easy harvesting while visually softening the structure of the fence.

Don't be dismayed if you contend with wildlife in your garden. A fence can be a beautiful addition and indeed a feature if you use a little creativity.

Disease

Diseases in the garden can occur once in a while or build up over time. Often their effects are minor, but in some years under certain conditions they can flourish and make a mess of things. Once again, prevention is key. Keeping the garden free of debris and weeds is number one. It's easy to do, prevents many diseases from cropping up, and keeps the garden looking better all around. Keeping plants healthy and interplanting a wide variety of plant families and species will also help prevent many diseases from becoming problematic.

Many garden diseases, primarily the fungal diseases like mildews, rusts, rots, and blights, can survive the winter on diseased plant debris or even in the soil. Therefore it is important to remove all dead plant material at the end of the year to prevent infection. Weeds also harbor some diseases and the insects that carry them, so freeing the garden of weeds will help prevent the onset and spread of diseases.

Strong plants fight off infection better than weak plants. Keeping plants healthy will help prevent infection even if the diseases are present in the garden. By providing fertile soil, balanced nutrients, proper light, adequate water, airflow, and growing space, the plants in your garden will likely be healthy and vigorous and will be able to fight off infection better than weak or poorly maintained plants.

When you're out and about in the garden, keep on the lookout for things that don't seem quite right. That way you'll find insect and disease problems early and have a better chance at managing them, like the powdery mildew on this zucchini plant.

Planting a wide variety of plants together creates an environment in which diseases cannot spread as easily. Most diseases are family-specific and often do not affect multiple plant families. All the ideas we've talked about throughout this book—companion planting, crop rotation, cover crops—apply here.

Pest insects, mammals, and diseases are a part of any garden, but don't have to become a major part of your gardening experience. Keeping things balanced, providing a healthy environment for your plants, mixing up plant families and species, and choosing plants that have particular resistance to problems, all go a long way to enjoying a long season in your garden.

HARVEST

Finally, it is time for harvest! You have prepared the soil, planted the seeds, tended the seedlings, nurtured the plants, watered, weeded, pinched, and pruned. You are well deserving of some reward, and some reward it is! Nothing compares to the sweet and tender flavors that come from the garden. In such a mixed garden, harvests are many and varied, beginning with sweet snap peas, crisp greens, peppery chives, and a few violas for the bud vase in early spring. As the weeks progress, the harvests grow more diverse: calendula petals yearn to sparkle on salads, blueberries and strawberries abound, fragrant herbs are everywhere. Finally, as the dog days settle in, the tomatoes and peppers ripen, providing the succulent flavors that define summer. Zucchini plants continue to offer more than we can possibly use, cucumbers dangle nonchalantly from their prickly vines, grapes begin to color, and peaches burst with sugary juices. A rainbow of blooms buzzes with bees and butterflies. Mixed with mint, parsley, dill, lavender,

Swiss chard can be harvested all season long by simply cutting the leaves off about an inch above the ground. A sharp knife works best to make a clean cut. The plants will continue to grow from the center, so every few days you'll have more leaves ready for harvesting.

Look beyond flowers to make gorgeous bouquets for the summer table. Herbs like parsley, dill, and cilantro make fragrant fillers, broccoli raab flowers add airy lightness, and borage lends a silver glow to a colorful combination of annual and perennial blooms.

and sage, these colorful flowers fill vases with intoxicating fragrance and the carefree appearance of a summer afternoon.

The harvest lasts for months, and every week the garden offers something new: a fresh mix of flavors, colors, and aromas to liven the spirit and the palate. As you carefully cut a few sturdy stems of chard for the evening's masterpiece, you can feel the satisfaction and joy of tending such a splendid and abundant piece of ground.

CHAPTER **5**

change of
seasons

During the long, sultry days of summer it's hard to imagine the season ever ending. We dream of summer lasting forever: steamy mornings when the sun sparkles through the haze of heat-drenched air; long days when the sun lingers into the late evening, sinking ever so slowly toward the horizon. It is an easy time to be a human. Our clothes are small, light, and cool, and we are unburdened by socks and shoes.

Just because summer is coming to an end doesn't mean the garden is finished. In early October, the last flush of peppers reflects the colors of autumn, along with nasturtium and crimson-hued dahlias.

107

The waning days of summer generally mean there's a lot of harvesting to be done. Tomatoes, especially, seem to keep producing longer than I ever expect. Keep a keen eye on your plants to be sure you don't miss any of these delicious gems. If you grow tired of harvesting, or a frost is coming, pick the remainders green and ripen them on the windowsill or use them green—there are many tasty uses for green tomatoes.

There's a sense of ease that comes with the summer. Schedules are looser, dress codes are relaxed, we stay up later, fun comes a little easier, and best of all, we get to play outside!

In the midst of it, I don't want it to end. Then a day comes when the air has a tinge of crispness—dry and fresh. And somehow, miraculously, it feels good. Suddenly there is this subtle shift in my mind. I start to look forward to cooler days, cooler nights. I picture the vibrant colors of the leaves, and the crackly sound of them crunching under my wool-socked-and-booted feet. I can actually imagine the feel of a thick sweater, a cozy scarf, a pillowy blanket. And finally, I can picture the peaceful dance of snowflakes as they descend gently to rest on the quiet trees.

IT'S NOT OVER YET

But just because a hint of fall is in the air doesn't mean the season of food and flowers is over in the garden. Before the snow brings on the silent, snuggly days of winter, there is much to be savored and enjoyed. As the days cool slightly, most plants will display renewed vigor. Those oppressive days of late summer, when many plants look thirsty and tired, can fool us into thinking the height of the season has passed. Yet, given a couple of cooler days, there are suddenly more ripe tomatoes than we know what to do with, the peppers grow more vibrant, and the greens perk up, fresh and crisp. Tender, warm-season favorites give it their last hurrah by producing as much as they possibly can, and we are the fortunate beneficiaries of this fervor. It seems like every time I turn around, another eggplant has appeared, another handful of beans is ready to pick.

While these plants are giving it everything they've got before the cold sets in, annual flowers, both edible and ornamental, that were looking weary and spent suddenly put forth a new flush of blooms. Signet marigolds regain their luminous lemon and tangerine glow. Calendula re-bloom fierce and fiery, distracting the eye from the knobby seed-heads left behind by the weary gardener. Violas, too, perk up and turn their bright faces to the sun. Zinnias, petunias, impatiens, and geraniums, all the classic annual flowers brighten and give the garden a fresh glow going into fall.

At the same time, other plants in the garden signal the onset of fall by drying out, turning from green to deep warm shades. The lofty dill, once fringed and feathery, fades to a dry copper. The seed-heads dry and burst open to sprinkle seed wherever the wind carries it. The scent of the plant transforms from herbal to earthy.

Dill looks beautiful in the garden as the cool days set in and the frilly green stalks turn a crisp copper hue. Before the seeds fall to the ground, collect them to use in the kitchen. Dill seeds have many wonderful uses from pickles to breads.
STUDIO BARCELONA/SHUTTERSTOCK

The blueberry bushes give us our second treat of the year by putting on a spectacular show of color. Never before have I seen a crimson so bright and pure as I have on a blueberry bush in fall. For this alone, blueberries would be worth having in the yard. The fact that they produce such delicious berries is a bonus!

Strawberries turn a mottled combination of green and red. The grape vine becomes a deep burgundy curtain. Color seems to be bursting from every corner of the garden, taking attention away from plants that are starting their slow decline. Each plant has its own season to shine, and thankfully some shine in the fall.

TIME FOR A FEW MORE SEEDS

While it seems counterintuitive at the time, late summer is the perfect time to get seeds started for some of those cool-loving fall crops. When the zucchini has become overgrown and wilted, it's the perfect time to pull those tired plants out and fill their space with the promise of crunchy greens, snappy radishes and sweet peas. The same plants that grow happily in the chilly days of spring will be comfortable, as the days grow shorter and cooler in the fall.

Cool-season plants grow quickly from seed sown right in the ground, meaning the empty spaces in your yard won't be empty for long. Within a few days of sowing radish seeds, tender green sprouts will emerge and grow almost before your eyes. After a few short weeks, the foliage will be filled in and the crisp roots will be swelling in the cool earth, their red crowns peeking out to let you know they're ready for picking.

Lettuce and other greens, being so easy and quick to grow, are the perfect way to add a splash of color to the late-season garden. Packets of lettuce seed usually contain many more seeds than I can use in my yard in the spring, so as late summer comes, I unfold the packets and sprinkle seed for ruby-red and lime-green lettuces wherever there's an empty spot that needs a little color. Within a month, the tender leaves are ready to snip. They'll remain surprisingly robust through the first couple of light frosts, but are some of the first cool-season veggies to succumb to harder frosts, especially the loose-leaf varieties. Romaine and other coarse lettuces may last a little longer.

Asian greens like pak choi and mizuna mustard tend to last a bit longer than the soft-leaved lettuces. Arugula handles the cold better still, and will keep growing until the first hard freeze. Arugula is full-grown in about forty days, but I can never wait to clip a few peppery leaves for my fall salad, so you can take a few outer leaves until it grows in fully.

Chard lasts a good long time in the fall, even after constant harvesting all season. Maybe it's me, but the bright colors of chard seem to intensify as the days grow cool. The deep red and orange stems mimic the colors of the changing leaves and give an autumnal look to the garden. I get a little more aggressive with my harvesting this time of year and cut more

As the garden is winding down for the season, you can start planning ahead for next year. Fall is the time to plant garlic, so be sure to think about next year's garden to ensure the fleshy, blue-green stalks will fit into a well-planned design.

and more leaves off the plants each time so as not to lose them to the cold.

Kale is the hardiest of the greens and will sometimes grow right on through winter if the temperatures aren't extremely low. The general consensus is that kale tastes best after it has experienced a few frosts, so I leave this one in longer than any other leafy green plant. The tough, leathery leaves seem untroubled by frosty nights and snowy days. If you don't mind trudging out through the snow to cut a few leaves, kale will reward you well into winter, giving garden-fresh goodness to winter salads and soups.

Broccoli and cauliflower grow surprisingly quickly and within two months can produce a good-sized head. If you have large spaces that have been left behind by zucchini or other warm season crops that have gone the way of the compost pile, plant a few of these heading crops to fill in the big gaps. Scattering seed of lightning-fast-growing calendula between will give the space some color while the vegetables mature. Heading plants fight off the cold with surprising ease and will tolerate a pretty stiff frost.

Many herbs will keep right on growing late into the season and some even into winter. Tender herbs, basil especially, will finish up early, but parsley will grow strong and proud all through fall. Sage, oregano, thyme, lavender, mint, chives, they'll be some of the last plants standing, which is great since you've probably started dreaming of rich stews and soups to make as the days grow cold.

THE SEASON COMES TO A CLOSE

Even the cool-season crops will eventually want to call it quits. And certainly, at some point you will agree with them. There's a definite shift that occurs, especially in northern regions, when we instinctively know it is time to prepare for winter.

It's a heavenly time to work outside. The sun in the fall takes on a golden cast, and nostalgia fills the air. Every brisk breeze that makes the leaves flutter and sprinkle down from the trees carries with it visions of country roads, pumpkin patches, scarecrows, and cornstalks. And with those visions, the scent of apples, roasted squash, and wood smoke. The silvery clouds hint at the biting days ahead, but the fresh,

Kale is one of those few annuals that will not succumb to the first frosts or even an early-season snow. Cold weather tends to improve the flavor of these rugged plants, so let them show their stuff through the first cold weeks, and you'll be able to reap the rewards. AUTHOR PHOTO

crimson, spicy, delicious fall is here and every moment outdoors is a gift to be savored.

How lucky we are that we have these tasks to fulfill at the end of every growing season. There's an innate satisfaction in cutting back, clearing out, tidying up, and putting away. I pull out my favorite sweatshirt and a sturdy pair of gloves, set some logs ablaze in the fire pit (for atmosphere), and get to work.

ANNUALS: CLEAN AND CLEAR

I definitely find it a good idea to err on the side of early when finally clearing out the garden for the winter. If very cold days are soon to come, I harvest the last of the cool-season edibles before they freeze. Not only do I want to avoid losing them to the cold, but it's a lot easier to pull the plants when they're still firm and crisp than when they're soggy and limp from having frozen. And it's a lot nicer to clean up the yard while it's dry and lovely than when everything is wet and slushy and my fingers are freezing.

Clear out all the annual plants and take them to the compost pile. There, the heat from the pile will kill most diseases that might be lingering on the plants. Rake out the annual beds and apply a layer of compost, and you'll be rewarded in the spring with a clean slate for planting your next masterpiece.

PERENNIALS: NEW LIFE IN WINTER

Perennials are a whole different story . . . well, mostly. Quite a few perennials look splendid in the garden throughout the winter. I'm not talking bright colors and blooms (not in the North anyway), I'm talking structure, form, and texture. And yes, color too. Although the color in a winter garden is much more subdued than the flashy color of summer, there is a surprising variety in the ecru, wheat, and umber shades that break the monotony of steel-gray skies and white snow.

During the growing season, perennials give foundation and permanence to the garden, and

The architecture of perennial plants becomes apparent in the winter when all the foliage has withered, and their visual value equals their value in the summer. Umbels and seed-heads collect snow and shimmer with frost, lending a magical appeal to the winter garden. GORDANA SERMEK/SHUTTERSTOCK

Many tender summer herbs can't make it through harsh northern winters. However, a few hardy herbs like thyme stand up to cold winters and look lovely while doing it. The fine stems and tiny leaves peek delightfully out of the snow, providing winter interest and allowing you to harvest a little. AUTHOR PHOTO

they do the same throughout the winter. Plus, they provide shelter and food for birds and other small creatures. And, they look great in the snow! Members of the aster family are some of my favorites, like echinacea (coneflower) and rudbeckia (black-eyed susan) with their large, dark seed-heads. Other asters, such as heath aster and New England aster, have bushier growth and fuzzy, tufted seed-heads that collect snow beautifully. Yarrow is another favorite of mine to keep throughout the winter. The bulk of the foliage dies back (or else I cut it back after a couple of good hard frosts) and what's left are fine stems topped with dense umbels that wear the snow like a jaunty cap. Grasses, rushes, and sedges look spectacular in winter, especially those with large seed spikes. Again, they provide food for birds and become sculptural in the pale light of winter. Of the edibles, I've always thought raspberries looked great in the winter. They generally drop their leaves and the bare canes arc playfully this way and that. Once dormant, you can thin the canes for a neater look, which will also make them ready to go in the spring.

For those perennials that remain in the garden throughout the winter, find some time in very early spring to cut them back before they start growing again. Get to them early so you don't damage any new growth.

CHANGE OF SEASONS

rotation

Different plant families use nutrients in different ways, are susceptible to different insects and diseases, and have root structures that vary. To maintain a healthy garden it's a great idea to mix up plant families. In the kind of garden we're talking about in this book, we're already mixing up plant families by interplanting all kinds of vegetables, fruits, herbs, and ornamentals together. This is a great formula for a healthy landscape. But if you tend to plant many of one kind of plant, for example, greens, tomatoes, or squash, you might want to try crop rotation.

Crop rotation is something we generally think of in relation to large-scale farming. One year there may be corn in a field, and the next it is replaced by soybeans. Rotation is an important practice because it helps moderate nutrient depletion in the soil, prevent insect pests and diseases, and promote good soil structure.

This practice can be as effective in the home landscape as it is on the farm, especially where insect pests and diseases are concerned. Rotating annual vegetable crops in the landscape helps keep problems at bay by moving the host crop around year after year. Many insects and diseases spend part of their life cycle in the soil, so if a host crop is in the same place year after year the pest will undoubtedly emerge and attack each year. But, if you rotate different families of plants over a three- or four-year period, chances are those diseases won't build up and the insect pests will not find their food source.

Rotation is not tricky and is easy to track by noting where plants are in the landscape each year. (This is a great use for the garden notebook.) If you plant zucchini every year, move it to a new area each year and put something else in last year's spot. It'll keep your landscape looking fresh and new and keep your plants healthier. Remember to rotate by plant family.

Of course, this is most important for annuals. Perennials that are well-maintained and healthy should be able to fight off many insect and disease problems. However, if problems appear and persist year after year, it is a good idea to pull the plants and start fresh in a new spot. This can be especially true for strawberries, which should be pulled and rotated after five years at the most.

Here's a chart of some landscape-friendly annual vegetables by family. Move plant families around the garden regularly to get the benefits of rotation.

Solanaceae
Eggplant
Pepper
Potato
Tomatillo
Tomato

Brassicaceae
Broccoli
Broccoli raab/rapini
Cabbage
Cauliflower
Kale
Mizuna mustard
Radish

Asteraceae
Artichoke
Endive
Lettuce

Alliaceae
Garlic
Leek
Onion

Cucurbitaceae
Cucumber
Melon
Winter squash
Zucchini

Apiaceae
Carrot
Dill
Parsley
Parsnip

Fabeaceae
Beans
Peas

Chenopodiaceae
Beet
Chard
Spinach

Without a thick covering of mulch, even the hardiest varieties of lavender may not survive the coldest winters. But I err on the side of beauty: the flower stalks look lovely topped with snow, so I tend not to mulch and hope the snow cover will provide some protection. The plants can be cut back by about a third in the spring, once new growth appears at the base. AUTHOR PHOTO

PERENNIAL HERBS FOR THE WINTER GARDEN

Many herbs are perennial in cooler regions and look great throughout the winter. Garden sage, in all but the very coldest areas, will stay relatively green through the winter. It shouldn't be harvested after September or so, because it needs to harden off for winter. Knowing that, however, I can't say that I haven't, from time to time, picked a few leaves in November to fry for a flavorful garnish or to chop up and sprinkle on a pork roast.

Thyme generally remains green too, and can be harvested with similar caution throughout the winter. Don't take too much, since the plant isn't actually growing at this time. You're actually doing dormant pruning by harvesting these herbs in winter. The tiny leaves on thyme's fine stems peek cheerfully out of the snow until the plant is buried, which in colder places will likely happen because of its short stature.

Lavender survives cold northern winters only sometimes. I don't go through huge efforts to save it every year by massively mulching it because, frankly, big clumps of mulch in my yard don't look so good. And if you haven't guessed it yet, a major point of all this is for it to look good—not only in the summer but all year long. Lavender grows surprisingly easily from seed, so I start some every spring, just in case. For this reason, I like to leave lavender as it is in the fall, all through the winter. The silvery foliage remains silvery. The spindly spikes poking through the snow make the winter garden magical.

PREPARING SOIL FOR NEXT YEAR

The soil in the garden provides a lot to plants throughout the growing season: moisture, nutrients, air, stability. Chances are the plants will use up a lot of the soil's resources, especially organic matter and nutrients. To keep plants healthy, the soil needs to be healthy, and after a season of giving it needs a little attention to get it bulked up and ready to provide for another season of lush plants and delicious food.

Cover Crops

When you think of cover crops you probably think of expansive farm fields, not garden beds. But the benefits of cover cropping in agricultural fields apply similarly to the home landscape and can even add visual appeal during the off-season. Cover crops are the little-known miracle workers of the garden world—humble plants that do wonders, but require little attention. A well-timed cover crop prevents erosion, deters weeds, improves soil structure, adds organic matter, and can even add nutrients to the soil.

Depending on the crop and location, cover crop seed can be sown in fall or spring, and certain crops have certain benefits. Leguminous (bean family) crops like hairy vetch, clover, and alfalfa have the special talent of converting air into nitrogen and locking it in the soil.

Planting a cover crop will not only add nutrients to the soil and prevent erosion, but will fill in the bare spots and provide some visual interest. A mix of cover crops like clover and lupine bursts with color while benefitting the soil. Hairy vetch, which also sports a purple flower, is commonly planted with clover in cooler regions. MARY TERRIBERRY/SHUTTERSTOCK

compost

Once upon a time when many people who grew vegetables and fruit also grew livestock of some kind, manure compost was ever-present and cheap. Free, really. This kind of diversified system created a balance of inputs and outputs that cycled naturally, back and forth. And it all happened on the same little piece of land that could be happily sustained for years and years. With a little effort on the part of the farmer, the livestock manure could be composted with yard waste or kitchen vegetable waste to create a rich soil amendment for use in the garden and in the fields and pastures.

Things are a bit different for most of us these days. Living in the city, many of us don't have large amounts of livestock manure lying around (probably a good thing), and to acquire it is often expensive. But composting yard waste and kitchen waste is easy to do, even in a small yard. Adding this compost to the soil in your yard will help build up organic matter in the soil, which will in turn stimulate microbial activity, improve the soil structure, and even add a few nutrients. It won't add as much nitrogen as manure compost, but the benefits of all that organic matter will help make the garden healthy and productive for both edibles and ornamentals.

Backyard composting is a great way to build your own (free!) soil amendment and reduce the amount of garbage you throw away, and it's easy and fun. It's a great way to teach kids about recycling, decomposition, and soil building. You don't necessarily need fancy, expensive containers nor do you need to spend a lot of time monitoring it. By alternately layering greens (fresh yard and kitchen waste) and browns (dry leaves and shredded wood) in a mound, keeping it moderately moist, and occasionally mixing it up, you will help hasten the breakdown of the materials into dark, rich humus. It will likely take several months to a year for this to happen, but once you get the process started it will become a continuous supply. The bins and tumblers made specially for composting may help speed up the process, but aren't necessary for making good compost. The Resources section suggests further sources of information on composting.

Talk about a handy plant for the garden! In most places these can be sown in early fall, when they'll grow a little, then they'll begin growth again in spring.

Winter rye and winter wheat can be planted in fall, later than the leguminous cover crops. These are good for gardeners who don't want to pull their edibles and ornamentals too early, or who simply don't get around to ordering seed in time. They start growing again in early spring, giving a fresh green cast to the garden before most other plants get started. These don't add nitrogen to the soil, but do offer all the other cover crop benefits. Rye is especially good at preventing weed growth. When it is tilled into the soil in spring, it releases chemicals as it decomposes. These chemicals prevent seeds from germinating. This is great for weeds, but not so great for small-seeded crops like lettuce or carrots. Be sure to till it in a good month before planting.

These are the hardiest of cover crops and will likely survive winters in colder areas. I prefer the idea of planting a cover crop in fall over spring, because in spring, the minute the ground thaws, I want to start planting cool-season veggies. I'd rather a cover crop do its work in the off-season so I don't have to sacrifice space in the spring.

All of these cover crops should be incorporated into the soil in the spring to add their organic matter and to make way for planting. Get to them early, before they have a chance to become too big and unwieldy. Hairy vetch can get, well, hairy, meaning long and tangled. Winter rye can become stout and tough to till in if left to grow too long. A few weeks after they've begun growth in the spring, mow and turn them into the soil.

Compost and Fertilizers

Fall is the perfect time of year to give the garden a good thick dose of compost. While the nutrient levels in compost are generally low, compost works its real magic promoting good soil structure, aiding moisture retention, and increasing microbial activity. These are all important and beneficial for a healthy, productive garden. Layering a couple of inches of well-rotted compost and turning it six to eight inches into soil can help lighten up hard, clay soils and, conversely, help add body and moisture-holding capacity to light, sandy soils. In any soil, the addition of compost boosts microbial activity, which is beneficial to plant growth.

Whether you're using purchased compost or compost you've made from yard and kitchen waste, it's often a good idea to mix some fertilizer into the compost when you apply it, since compost is generally low in nutrients, especially nitrogen. Organic choices for higher-nitrogen fertilizers mainly come from plant and animal byproducts. Some plant byproducts that provide a good source of nitrogen include corn gluten meal, cottonseed meal, and soybean meal. High nitrogen animal byproducts include blood meal, bat guano, fishmeal or emulsion, and dried manure from poultry and cattle. There

Spreading compost is an enjoyable autumn activity and helps to boost the nutrient content of the soil. A simple screen can be used to filter out large particles, like sticks that don't break down quickly and would make digging difficult in spring.

are a growing number of certified-organic fertilizers on the market that contain a mixture of many of these items in various combinations for specific nutrient needs. Always read instructions carefully to be sure you choose the right combination and use the product safely.

Take some time to read up on and understand compost and fertilizers from some of the resources included in the back of this book. When you understand a bit about how they work, you'll be able to make good choices and find they work much better for your garden. It's interesting stuff, the science behind organic matter and nutrients, and how they work in the soil and in plants. With a little extra knowledge, the mysteries of your garden may not be quite so mysterious.

PRUNING

Mid- to late-winter is the time to think about pruning. Pruning seems like a daunting task, but with a few rules in mind, it can be quite easy, quick, and satisfying. We prune to help the plant stay healthy and productive and keep it looking its best.

When woody plants are left to their own devices, they put on so much growth they can actually damage themselves. Branches overlap, stressing each other; foliage becomes too dense, preventing light and air from moving through, leading to disease and decline; flower buds become too numerous, reducing the size and quality of the fruits they'll become. Too much growth can lead to breakage, creating entry points for damaging insects and pathogens.

At the same time, woody plants don't necessarily have aesthetics in mind when they grow. They'll send branches out this way and that, some straight up, some straight down, some longer than all the rest. Some plants will sucker, sending new shoots up from the ground, attempting to spread, regardless of the space you have allotted them. Some will simply try to grow too large.

With careful pruning we can help our trees and shrubs remain healthy while simultaneously bending them to our aesthetic will. And it doesn't have to be complicated. The first rule of thumb: anything that looks diseased, damaged or dead should go. Then, by taking a few moments to look at the plant you will probably be able to see the major problems, and likely be able to imagine what you want it to look like when you're done. In general, you want to create a balanced plant with plenty of space for air to flow and new growth to fill in. There are many detailed resources in books and online to help guide you to a properly pruned plant. I've included some of these resources in the back of this book. The most important thing to remember: don't be afraid to prune. Pruning actually stimulates growth, and the chances of your pruning too aggressively are low. Most of us don't prune nearly enough. Follow some reliable guidelines and see how it goes. Each year you'll learn a little more, and soon pruning will be an easy task you look forward to.

MAKING PLANS

During the long quiet months of winter, when the garden rests and regenerates, and thoughts of spring start to flicker here and there, it is the perfect time for the gardener to reflect on the past season. Crack open the garden notebook, which by this time is probably filled with sketches, photos, notes, print-outs from helpful websites, and pages torn from seed catalogs and magazines. Peruse through and you'll be reminded of ideas you had throughout the season: plant combinations that worked particularly well, and those that didn't; varieties that looked great and produced well, and some that fell short of expectations; problems that occurred like diseases, insects, or wildlife. You may have had ideas about adding edibles to a new spot in the yard, a great trellis idea for your tangled tomatoes or wandering cucumbers, and countless other creative visions that came to you throughout the season.

It is exciting and inspiring to be reminded of all these things and start planning for spring. You might be ready to expand, to add a few perennials, to prepare a special spot for blueberries or fruit trees. This is the time for imagination, for taking what you've learned from your garden and building upon it or simply

Looking back through pictures of the previous season might remind you of plant combinations that worked particularly well, such as this colorful trio of cosmos, kale, and calendula. The pink cosmos blossoms picked up the pink in the kale veins, while the bright yellow calendula flowers popped out above the rest.

refining it. The wonderful thing about gardens is that every year is a clean slate, a blank canvas on which we can experiment, try new ideas. If they work we build on those, if they don't we reconfigure and try again.

Gazing out over the clean, white snow you may find your mind filling with visions of lush greens sparkling with dew, sweet fragrances of lavender and sage, and flowers buzzing with bees and butterflies. With these visions ripe in your mind, get out that pencil and grab a few fresh pages for this year's notebook. After all, spring is just around the corner.

TOP: Make plans to try new and exciting color and texture combinations to create visual excitement in the garden. A row of fleshy green chard between tall pink nicotiana and low-growing bright orange zinnias creates a striking and unexpected combination.

BOTTOM: Don't forget to include plants for the bees and other garden helpers. Borage is a gorgeous addition to the landscape and will keep those pollinators coming to the garden all season.
AUTHOR PHOTO

favorite plants
for the
edible landscape

KUTTELVASEROVA/SHUTTERSTOCK

Artichoke
Cynara cardunculus
There's nothing quite as striking as artichoke in a landscape. The jagged silver foliage makes anything near it look soft and delicate. It's a great contrast with almost any colorful, softer-textured plant. Growing three to four feet tall, these members of the thistle family produce edible flower buds if given enough time. This can be challenging in areas with shorter seasons because the plant generally takes about six months to produce buds. You can overcome this problem in northern climes by choosing varieties with shorter bloom times and by starting seed indoors in late winter. Root divisions are a great way to start artichoke plants, if they're available in your area. If you do get a crop, be sure to leave a couple of the buds on and let them flower for a spectacular sight.

In warmer climates artichoke is a perennial, producing well for five or six years, after which point it should be divided. In such a climate, the first year is usually devoted to root growth, meaning buds are removed. If you're going for maximum production, this may be a good choice. Overwintering involves cutting the plants back to the ground and applying a thick layer of mulch.

This unusual vegetable can be steamed, baked, boiled, and grilled. The tender hearts are used on pizzas and in any number of Mediterranean dishes. I think they're best simply prepared by steaming and served whole with a lemon butter sauce: simple and delicious!

123

Asparagus

Asparagus officinalis

I am a relatively impatient gardener, which is why I have never grown asparagus. But I absolutely love eating asparagus, so I am getting closer and closer to finally planting it. That said, asparagus, for the patient gardener, makes a nice landscape plant. Asparagus is one of the few vegetable plants that is a perennial even in cooler regions. In fact, healthy plants in a weed-free plot will produce for about fifteen years. In its edible state, there's not a whole lot to see because its tender stalks are so delicious they simply don't last long before being harvested. But after harvesting is done in the spring, asparagus grows tall and ferny, providing a lovely backdrop to the landscape. This may pose a bit of a challenge when deciding on placement. Generally, the taller the plant the farther back it should be placed. But access is

critical in the spring to harvest all those delicious stalks. Thankfully at the time asparagus is producing its harvestable crop, most other plants won't be filled in yet, so a few well-placed steppingstones provide easy access.

The light and airy foliage of asparagus once it has "ferned out" makes an exquisite backdrop to many plants. Calendula is a colorful front for asparagus, and may help deter some pests. For best results, buy one-year-old crowns to get an earlier crop. Be sure to buy male plants, since the females will drop seed and become weedy. Both male and female plants will produce edible spears, but generally the male plants produce many more because the plants do not have to put so much energy into seed production. Look for purple varieties for something a bit different. The color fades to green when cooked, but the purple varieties have a distinct flavor that you won't find in grocery store asparagus.

Beans

Phaseolus vulgaris or
Phaseolus coccineus

Nothing matches the deliciously crispy snap of a bean direct from the garden. And few food plants give you quick-growing foliage and season-long bloom like beans. Bush beans certainly have their place in the landscape, but my favorite to grow are vining pole beans for two reasons: one, their vining stems grow quickly to cover trellises with soft, heart-shaped leaves; and two, they

FOODPICTURES/SHUTTERSTOCK

produce a lot more in a given space than bush beans do.

One of my favorites is the scarlet runner bean. This one grows quickly and produces bright red flowers, which mature into green bean pods. The beans are best when picked small, young, and tender, and if you pick them regularly, you'll encourage more spectacular blossoms. Another perk: the flowers are edible too! If you simply can't wait for the beans themselves, pick a few flowers to put in a green salad for a splash of color. There are hundreds of varieties of beans to choose from, whether you're going for fresh or dried beans. Look for varieties with some visual flair like purple pods, or the striped and speckled pods of 'Rattlesnake'. If you're looking for an interesting trellising idea, try the traditional "three sisters" technique of growing corn, beans, and squash. The beans climb up the corn, and the squash fills

STANJOMAN/SHUTTERSTOCK

in the space around the base. This method makes for a great conversation piece.

Beans should be direct-sown after the soil has warmed at the base of a trellis or whatever structure you plan to let them climb on. Keeping them up on a trellis will help to keep the leaves dry, preventing some disease issues that come with wet foliage. Full sun is best for heavy bloom, but a little shade is okay. Remember, plants in part shade won't be as vigorous and yield may be lower.

Broccoli raab
Brassica ruvo

Also known as rapini, Italian broccoli, or Chinese broccoli, this is a fast-growing, cool-season relative of broccoli that produces smaller stems with florets at the top that can be harvested little by little through the season. This slender, upright plant is great to use in the landscape and is a more versatile plant than heading broccoli. Heading broccoli takes up a lot of space for a long period of time, and once you harvest, that's all you get. Then you have a huge void where the plant was. Alternatively, broccoli

raab takes up a very small amount of space and can be seeded every couple of weeks for a continual harvest all season. After it flowers, the flavor diminishes, so pull the plants and reseed, or leave the flowers and you'll delight in the number of beneficial insects they attract.

Broccoli raab has a distinct flavor, like broccoli but a little bitter, and is delicious sautéed in a bit of olive oil or butter. Added to stir-fry dishes it offers a bright broccoli flavor. Sautéed with a bit of bacon, broccoli raab is quite a treat. I've even made pesto with it after I've harvested a large amount. Add some basil, Parmesan, pine nuts, and olive oil, and you've got a surprisingly delicious sauce for pasta or pizza.

Flea beetles seem to love this plant and tend to do some damage early in the season. Generally the plants can survive this; they may simply be a little lacy looking for a while. Cabbage worms, root maggots and aphids also tend to pester these plants, but plant enough in various locations and you should be able to outsmart the little devils.

Carrots
Daucus carota

Carrots do most of their magic below ground, naturally. It's too bad we can't normally see the bright colors of those nutritious roots, especially since so many vivid colored varieties are available: golden, purple, red, amazing! But with all that goodness underground, we get to take advantage of two levels

of the landscape. While those roots are maturing out of sight, the gorgeous, frilly green foliage adds lightness to the landscape. This is a nice contrast to bolder-textured, bigger leaved plants like lettuce. Vertical, fleshy onions may also provide contrast to the carrot, especially if root veggies are a theme.

One challenge of any root veggie in the landscape is the void it creates when harvested. If these empty spaces a couple of times a year would detract from your landscape, there are a few things you can do. Successive planting of carrot seeds over a couple of weeks will mean a longer range of harvest and a bed that's never empty. Interplanting with spreading herbs or ornamental annuals that will fill in the gaps when the carrots are harvested is a foolproof way to prevent bald spots in the landscape midseason.

Carrots are easy to grow from seed and do best when seeded

directly into the garden bed in the spring. When the plants are a few inches tall, pull out the smaller, weaker-looking ones, leaving the hearty ones about an inch or two apart. They prefer light, loose soil and will produce the straightest roots in these conditions. A few pests cause some trouble for carrots like carrot root flies, leaf hoppers, and flea beetles, but are usually not a huge problem. Keeping your landscape clean and weed-free with plenty of air circulation can help prevent problems. Scattering carrot plantings around the landscape will likely mean if some are affected, others will be safe.

Celery
Apium graveolens var. *dulce*
Few people think of celery as anything other than the pale, leafless stalks tucked inside plastic bags in the produce section, neatly arranged in a stack, barely resembling plants. When a recipe suggests using celery

leaves to add flavor, we have only the tiny leaf remnants left at the very top, which is a shame because the leaves do indeed add a wonderfully deep flavor. Growing your own will remedy this problem and allow you to see what a fabulous plant celery is. First you'll find that celery is a deep green, not pale and white like we see in the grocery store (most commercially grown celery is blanched in the fields to give it this pale color and to make the flavor milder). You'll also find it is topped with big, shiny, parsley-like leaves.

Because of its stick-straight stalks, celery is a unique plant to use in the landscape, adding a distinct verticality despite its relatively short stature. It works well as a midrange plant and pairs nicely with airy ornamentals like cosmos and gaura (both non-edible). Nasturtium tumbling its way among celery plays off the rigidity of its neighbor, looking carefree and lively. Celery planted at the base of a tomato plant lends a sturdy foundation and helps to hide late-season bare-tomato-stem syndrome.

Celery is a slow grower, so it's best to start it indoors in late winter or early spring. Celery loves cool weather, so plant it out early (be sure to harden it off first). It can handle a bit of shade, particularly if the growing season is extremely hot. Celery can be harvested a bit at a time throughout the season by gently breaking off a few of the outer stalks.

Chard
Beta vulgaris
Chard, or Swiss chard, is my number-one favorite edible landscaping plant. This beet relative is very easy to grow and has very few pest problems. Different varieties produce plants in a veritable rainbow of colors. The stems (or more specifically the leaf petioles) range in color from pure white, through yellow and orange, all the way to deep burgundy. The leaf blades are green in all varieties, but span from pale emerald through deep, almost purple-green. And the texture of the leaves varies a bit too, from relatively smooth to deeply wrinkled.

Chard prefers full to part sun, but will grow in shadier conditions as well. With less sun, however, it will grow a little slower and the color will be less intense. The leaves grow from a central crown, creating an upright-mounded form about eighteen inches tall. This makes

the plant perfect for use in borders so you can see the bright stems. Chard also works well as a midrange plant, with shorter herbs or annuals planted in front. Chard looks great planted with parsley, thyme, and sage, colorful ornamentals like zinnias (which pick up the stem colors) or fluffy alyssum. Keep in mind textures and habits that might contrast nicely with the rugged leaves and stick-straight stems of the chard.

Chard is technically a cool-season vegetable, but it grows well throughout the season and tends not to bolt because of its biennial nature. It is one of those few greens that will be content and colorful right through the dog days of summer and on into the chilly days of autumn. Harvest chard all season long by cutting outer leaves about an inch above the base. When young and small, the leaves are great in salads. When larger, the leaves are delicious used in any recipe that calls for spinach, adding more body and flavor. The colorful stems are certainly edible and should not be discarded as many recipes suggest. Chop them up and add them to the pan a few minutes before the leaves to soften them up. Try chard in stir fry, lasagna, frittatas, tarts, and sautes.

Cucumbers
Cucumis sativus
Homemade pickles and fresh cucumber salad are special treats from the summer garden, and thankfully they come from interesting-looking and easy-to-

AUTHOR PHOTO

grow plants. Cukes will do best if they're given something to climb on, which is always a great opportunity to get some height into the garden. They'll do well on a simple teepee made of a few long bamboo stakes or even thin tree branches. Wrapping the teepee with twine, wire, or something similar in a spacing of eight inches or so will create more support for the vine and the fruits. Trellising in this way allows for lots of air circulation, exposes flowers to pollinators, and provides plenty of space and support. Other trellising options will work as well, and cucumbers are a handy plant to camouflage a chain-link fence.

When shopping for seeds, don't stop at the classic green pickling and slicing cukes. Look around for unusual varieties to spice up your landscape and dinner table: long and slender, round, and in colors like yellow and white.

Powdery mildew can be a problem later in the season, causing yellow spots, gray leaves,

and unripe fruits. To avoid this, maintain good air circulation within your plants, keep the area under the plants clean and free of weeds and dead plant material, and if you do see the first few signs of powdery mildew, clip out the affected leaves to slow the spread. Also, look for disease-resistant varieties.

Eggplant
Solanum melongena
Eggplant is a staple of the edible landscape, not only for its delicious fruits, but also for its interesting form and colors. The plants have open, airy architecture, with branched stems and soft green leaves, and they are generally self-supporting, needing no staking or trellising, though some of the heavier-fruited varieties may need support later in the season. The plants grow to about two or three feet with space underneath to grow colorful trailing annuals, herbs, or even strawberries.

The best part about growing eggplant is the choice of shapes and colors of the fruits themselves: Tiny fingerlings in deep purple or white (look for 'Hansel' and 'Gretel'), small globes in blushed pinks and lavenders (try 'Rotunda Bianca' or 'Round Mauve'), stripes of white and purple ('Pandora Striped Rose' or 'Calliope'), speckles of green and white (Thai varieties), long and curved white, green, and purple, ribbed orange, and the classic deep aubergine monsters. Page through a seed catalog and you may be overwhelmed by the choices. Heirloom varieties with seductive names like 'Violette di Firenze' and 'Rosa Bianca' are hard to resist. The white-fruited varieties are surprising in the landscape and delicious in the kitchen, with mild and creamy flavors. These varieties often have spectral names like 'Ghostbuster' and 'Casper'. These more unusual varieties are worth the effort of starting the seeds at home, since plants of these varieties are not often found in garden centers.

Hops
Humulus lupulus
Here's a tricky one to classify. The most commonly used part of the hop plant is its resinous flower, which really isn't all that edible until dried and boiled as part of the brewing process or steeped as a tea. On the other hand, its tender green shoots that arise from spreading underground rhizomes, can be used like a vegetable.

Hops are becoming popular for home gardens, not only for their role in homebrewing, but also for their value as a landscape plant. Hops are a fast-growing, long-lived, perennial vining plant able to grow as much as twenty feet in a season, perfect for disguising an ugly fence or garage wall. Keep in mind hops need something to grasp onto, so if you grow them along a wall, build a trellis or provide strings or wires for them to twine around. Hops are striking when grown on a decorative obelisk, an arbor, or a pergola. The dense foliage follows the form of the structure with sculptural grace, and the pale green cones (the hops themselves), which are actually clusters of female flowers, dangle in perfect view for harvesting.

Throughout the season, hops can be tip-pruned to maintain shape and size. Beware, though, the leaves and stems are quite rough and irritating to the skin, so gloves and long sleeves are a good idea when training, pruning, and harvesting. Speaking of harvesting, not only are the cones used for brewing,

they also have been traditionally used to help treat insomnia, similar to chamomile and lavender. Dried and made into a tea or used to fill a pillow, hops are known to have a calming effect. For a special treat in the spring, snip a few tender shoots and prepare like you would asparagus. They have a similar flavor with a hint of bitterness. Also try pickling the shoots for a unique and flavorful snack.

Hops spread via rhizomes, so you'll want to keep on top of pruning those back. Aphids and spider mites can cause some trouble on this plant but are usually easily controlled by strong sprays of water. Avoid using insecticidal oils or soaps, since these may also harm the beneficial insects present on the plant.

Kale
Brassica oleracea
Kale is a relative of cabbage and broccoli and is considered to be one of the most nutritious vegetables on the planet. Even

better, kale is a great-looking plant that lends itself well to the edible landscape because of its interesting texture and silvery hues. This cool-season favorite is easily started from seed as soon as the soil is thawed enough to be worked. The small, spherical seeds send up seedlings quickly in the early days of spring. Kale does best in full to part-sun, but will tolerate some shade, though it will be less robust. Kale has few disease or pest problems, the most common being aphids that healthy plants can usually fight off without too much trouble. Syrphid flies and lady beetles residing in your garden help to defend kale against these aphids, but if those don't do the trick, give the aphids a hearty spray from the hose to knock them off the plants.

Many varieties of kale offer a broad range of leaf shapes and colors. 'Dinosaur', also known as 'Lacinato' or 'Tuscan' kale, has a long, slender leaf on a plant that resembles a miniature palm tree. The silvery-blue color is unique and lends a touch of smoky mystery to the landscape. This color and the leathery texture make 'Dinosaur' a stunning companion to softer, lighter textured, and brightly colored plants. 'RedBor' is a garden classic, with frilly leaves that have purple-red veins. As the weather cools in the fall, the entire plant takes on a redder hue, still with that silvery tinge common to all types of kale. One of my favorites is 'Red Russian', which has a purple-green color and a leaf shape somewhere between 'Dinosaur' and 'RedBor'. The color is most intense in early spring and autumn.

To harvest, trim outer leaves throughout the season, or wait until the first few frosts when the flavor sweetens. Use the leaves in salads, soups, and sauteed and stir-fried dishes. A deliciously simple way to prepare kale is to saute it in a little olive oil or butter, adding a dash of vinegar right at the end. Sprinkled with salt and pepper, this is a surprisingly tasty and very nutritious side dish.

Lettuce and other greens
Lactuca spp., *Eruca* spp. and *Brassica* spp.

There are so many varieties of lettuce out there that it would take an entire book to cover them all. Heading varieties can be interesting additions to the landscape, but I prefer the loose-leaf varieties that can be harvested little by little throughout the season. A zillion different leaf shapes and colors ranging from pale green to deep purple, speckled or spotted, make lettuces a great cool-season alternative to annual flowers. Or better yet, a companion to annual flowers!

TINYDEVIL/SHUTTERSTOCK

Lettuces and other salad greens are great space fillers and border plants in a landscape. Mizuna mustard has a unique, fringed texture, and adds a zippy flavor to salads. Osaka purple mustard has a spoon-shaped leaf and a deep purple color with lime-green veins. This is a stunner in the landscape and can be used in salads and cooking all season. Arugula is a salad classic, and its soft green leaves add a calm green to borders. Harvest all these greens throughout the season by clipping off a few of the outer leaves. Lettuces tend to bolt as the weather warms, so be sure to sow seeds successively or allow flowering annuals to fill in the spaces left when the lettuces are ready to come out. To slow bolting, give these plants a little shade. A great method is to plant lettuces under a trellis or teepee where the climbing plants will offer a bit of shade as the season progresses. If you don't mind the flower stalks in the design of your landscape, the flowers of lettuce, arugula and mustard are also edible. These diminutive flowers are great at attracting beneficial insects to the garden. Their thin stems and airy, pale flowers are also beautiful in flower arrangements.

Malabar spinach
Basella alba

Malabar spinach, or Ceylon spinach, is a relative newcomer to the temperate garden, but it is quickly finding a solid place in the edible landscape. This vining plant is unrelated to spinach

(*Spinacia oleracea*), but can be used similarly. In cooler temperatures it tends to creep slowly. When the heat is turned on it will start growing vigorously, and cover a trellis in no time. This is the climber to use in that hot spot in your yard. Keep your eyes open for the red-stemmed variety: the red is a gorgeous contrast to the deep, shiny green leaves.

In the kitchen lies the kicker: unlike spinach, this guy has a texture issue. Some people don't mind it at all; some people hate it. And that texture is slimy: think okra slimy. Wait, don't stop reading yet. It is such a great looking plant, and it happens to be super-nutritious, even including protein! If you grow it and find the texture doesn't agree with you in salads and lightly cooked situations, try it in a soup where it will add thickness as well as color and a lot of nutrients. It is traditionally used in Indian and Asian cooking, so look for recipes from these regions to find the best uses.

When harvesting, it is a bit tedious to pick leaf by leaf. To make harvest go a little faster, clip twelve inches or so off the end of the stems (the tender stems are edible too). This will promote branching and save you a lot of time.

Okra
Abelmoschus esculentus
Okra is a fascinating plant, guaranteed to cause a stir in your landscape, especially in the North where it is completely unexpected. This hibiscus relative produces showy flowers like its ornamental cousin, usually in pale, creamy hues of yellow and pink with a deep burgundy center. The red varieties are the most striking in the landscape and will produce edible pods after about fifty days. The plants are upright, about three to five feet tall, with an airy architecture of sturdy stems and large palmate leaves. Red okra looks great planted near green plants like kale, lettuce, and peppers. Ornamentals like zinnia or nicotiana (both non-edible) provide a contrast of texture and color.

Okra does well direct-sown after the soil has warmed completely and risk of cold weather is past. In the North, it is best to start this one indoors in early spring to get a jump on the season and prevent any cold damage. Okra loves sunny, hot conditions, so plant it in that spot where most other plants would wither from the heat. The flashy flowers will develop into pods almost overnight, so keep an eye out for them and pick them while they're small and tender, about three to four inches long. Keep picking and it'll keep producing.

Many know okra only as a fried treat or an ingredient in gumbo, but it is so much more versatile. It's delicious roasted or sauteed with a little bacon, and in classic dishes with greens, tomatoes, or corn. Okra is also used in Indian and African cooking.

Peppers
Capsicum annuum
The bright colors and widely varied shapes of the pepper make it an obvious choice for the landscape. It's exciting to see a ripe orange pepper peeking through the airy foliage. In fact, it's difficult to hold back when exploring variety options since there are so many to choose from: fat, crispy-sweet bells; long, slender Italian fryers; and tiny, fiery chilis. They all look so fabulous, how is one to choose? I try to stick with varieties that I will actually eat, and even though the wildly hot ones are wildly appealing, I know I

probably won't use them much. There are, however, countless sweet varieties that prove just as beguiling. There are tiny red sweet pimentos, delicate sweet bananas, and baby bells in red, golden, and chocolate (deep purple-brown).

Peppers are easy to grow from seed, and can be started indoors in cooler regions to get a jump on the season. Pepper plants make good landscape specimens, individually planted with other species surrounding. This shows off their good looks and helps prevent widespread pest problems. There are a number of insect pests that can damage peppers, so plant them in various places throughout the garden, and you may outsmart the pests. Peppers do well planted somewhat tightly with other plants because they enjoy higher humidity, protection from wind, and a little shade on the fruits. Planted with some sturdy companions for support, peppers will not require staking. They generally thrive when planted with tomatoes,

chives, and other herbs. Trailing petunias (non-edible) add a nice touch, filling in the understory with soft color.

Tomatos
Solanum lycopersicum
What is a garden without tomatoes? Few gardeners can resist the plethora of sizes, shapes, colors, and flavors of this succulent summer staple. The delight that comes from a freshly picked tomato makes us forget the tangled mess that is a typical tomato plant. Countless creations have been devised to support these unruly plants—cages, ladders, spirals—all kinds of contraptions that promise to be the answer to tomato plant terror. The plants seem to grow before your eyes, and if you forget to put a cage around them in time, trying to wrestle them into submission often results in broken stems and dropped fruits.

So, what to do with these in the edible landscape to rein

them in and make them a visual treat as well as the tasty kind? Think trellising, and think creatively. Keep in mind that for part of the season, the plants will be small and most of what you'll see is the support system. You don't want to look out on ugly rusted tomato cages, do you? But what about a wrought-iron or wood garden obelisk? These structures, traditionally used to support flowering vines like clematis or thunbergia, offer eye-catching support to indeterminate tomatoes. But don't stop there, imagine tiny cherry tomatoes cascading from an arbor, or rambling along the garden fence. An antique metal headboard would be an unexpected sight in a cottage-style garden and would offer lots of support to a twining tomato.

Think also about plantings around the base of the tomatoes. Usually, late in the season, the leaves at the base of a tomato plant will turn brown and limp, leaving the stem bare and gnarly. A few well-placed plants will hide this immodesty and add a pop of color. Since the marigold is a classic tomato companion, try the 'Signet' or 'Gem' varieties (*Tagetes tenuifolia*) with their mounds of tiny orange, yellow, and red flowers. Or plant some purple basil and other herbs, colorful trailing nasturtium, or bee balm to attract a lot of pollinators. And don't forget to move your tomatoes to a new spot every year to prevent the buildup of diseases in the soil.

Zucchini

Cucurbita pepo

Zucchini is the squash of choice for the edible landscape because of the availability of bush-types that don't require much space. Some of the yellow squash varieties claim to be bush-type, but the ones I've grown always end up being larger than I have space for. I've had the best luck with zucchini. The impressive size and habit of the zucchini plant make it a striking specimen in the landscape. Usually one plant will suffice to feed a family for the summer.

Choosing the right spot for zucchini might be tricky and deserves some forethought. It's rather tall at three to four feet, so it seems a good choice to fit in the center or back of a bed, but you need good access to the plant to harvest those sneaky zucchini that have a tendency to hide under the big leaves until they're two feet long and the flavor becomes bland. A few well-placed

steppingstones will help you get in there to search for tender, young zucchini. Another great solution is to grow zucchini in a large container. I've had success with this, since it gets the plant up off the ground where there's better air circulation (which helps ward off pesky diseases like powdery mildew) and it puts the delicious fruits within easy reach, usually hanging delicately over the edges of the container. A half-barrel or similar size container should do the trick.

FRUITS

Apples

Malus domestica

Apple trees have changed a lot since my early days visiting apple orchards in the fall. Back then the trees were large and gnarly, and most fruit was far out of reach from the ground. These huge trees were difficult for the average gardener to harvest from and prune, mainly because of their large size.

Enter the dwarf apple tree. Over the past thirty years or so, apple breeders have been working on ways to make apple trees smaller, primarily for efficiency in commercial orchards. It's faster, safer, and easier to pick, prune, and otherwise manage eight-foot trees than thirty-foot trees. This is an advantage for home growers as well. Now we can easily reach all the fruit, prune and thin with ease, and even fit a few varieties in a small yard.

Most apple varieties sold to home growers these days are on semi-dwarfing or dwarfing rootstocks, but you should talk with the nursery to be absolutely sure. You don't want to plant a tree assuming it's going to be eight feet tall and end up with an enormous standard-size tree.

Apples require cross-pollination, so it is often suggested that a gardener plant more than one variety in the yard. But with the abundance of crab apple trees in most residential areas, chances are the pollinators will visit those as well as your tree.

I won't lie to you: apples have their share of problems, and some varieties are more finicky than others. This shouldn't scare you away from growing them in your yard, though, because they are nice-looking trees and there's a special joy about being able to pick fruit right from your own yard. Get off on the right foot by getting a variety that is hardy in your region. Check with orchards in your area and see which varieties they've had the most success with. They may even give you a few pointers on growing a good tree.

Blueberry
Vaccinium spp.

Every yard should have a few blueberry bushes. Touted by nutritionists as a super-food, and consistently placed in top-ten lists of foods you should eat every day, blueberries are packed with nutrients and flavor. But even better, the plant they grow on is attractive, is easy to manage, and boasts spectacular fall color.

Blueberries are native to the United States, and there's a variety for almost every climate. Sizes vary from the lowbush varieties, which can be a foot tall, to the highbush varieties that can grow to eight feet. No matter the variety, blueberry bushes have a naturally rounded form and attractive branching. The small, ovate leaves are dark and shiny and in the fall become a stunning kaleidoscope of gold, orange, crimson, and burgundy.

Blueberries are long-lived (thirty to fifty years!) and easy to manage, provided you meet one important need: they must be grown in acidic soil (pH 4.0-5.0). Planting them in a peat-soil mix is a good start. Smaller varieties do well in containers, so try this if you can't get your garden soil acidic enough. Blueberries

SUSAN MCKENZIE/SHUTTERSTOCK

require cross-pollination to set lots of juicy fruit, so plant a couple of varieties near each other. You'll be amazed at the differences in flavor among varieties! Prune the bushes every couple of years to maintain good shape and vigor. And finally, don't worry too much about insects or disease. Blueberries have few issues with these if planted in the right soil and pruned regularly.

Citrus
Citrus spp.

If I lived in the South I would grow a wide variety of citrus. I lived in the Caribbean for half a year and it was a special treat to be able to pick limes off the tree in the backyard for tropical drinks, desserts, and marinades. I envy those of you who can grow citrus, not only for the delicious fruit, but for the stately evergreen trees and intoxicating flowers. The trees respond well to pruning and can be shaped to particular forms and trained as espaliers.

Sadly for those of us in the North, citrus trees are severely damaged if exposed to below-freezing temperatures for more than two or three hours. While we cannot grow citrus in the ground, we can grow containerized citrus for an unexpected treat. Many varieties are available as dwarf trees, making them perfect for containers. 'Meyer' lemon and 'Kaffir' lime are two popular dwarf varieties. In fact, the leaves of the 'Kaffir' lime tree are used in some Asian cooking, so you can use both the leaves and the fruit.

DARKO PLOHL/DREAMSTIME.COM

Light, of course, is the critical factor when growing citrus in containers, because, for part of the year these plants will be indoors. Give them eight hours of high-quality light in a warm location (55–85 degrees F), supplementing with full spectrum grow lights if necessary. When the days (and nights) warm in the spring, take your container tree outdoors to add a spark of the tropical to your landscape.

Cranberry
Vaccinium macrocarpon

Cranberries, contrary to popular belief, are not grown in water. If you've seen pictures of cranberry fields, often termed

LIJUAN GUO/SHUTTERSTOCK

"bogs," flooded with water, then you've seen pictures of harvest. Cranberries float, and in commercial production a common method of harvesting is to flood the field and then go through with a machine that pulls or knocks the berries off their vines. The berries float to the top and are easily corralled and loaded into a truck. This is a lot faster than the traditional method of walking through a field raking the berries into a basket. It was backbreaking work, because cranberries grow on very low vines along the ground, only a few inches high.

All of this means anyone can grow cranberries at home, as there's no need for a bog of any kind. Cranberries actually prefer sandy, well-drained, acidic soil. The diminutive plants have tiny oval leaves and spread by runners. Cranberry can be grown as a ground cover and also makes a lovely container plant. The runners usually grow about a foot or two during a season, so imagine them cascading over the edges of a mixed container. Midseason you'll see flowers resembling a crane's head (the name evolved from crane berry to cranberry), and by early fall you'll be harvesting your own ruby-red berries just in time for Thanksgiving!

Cranberries are best started from cuttings, which are available for purchase from several fruit nurseries, and can generally be ordered online and shipped directly to you.

Currant and gooseberry
Ribes spp.

Your experience with currants may be those shriveled little black things in the scone you buy at your neighborhood coffee shop or in preserves so laden with sugar that you can't even discern the flavor of the currant. But have you ever plucked a string of ruby-red berries off the bush and tasted the tangy-sweet juiciness of a perfectly ripe currant? Let me tell you . . . it is like sunshine in your mouth!

The currant and its cousin, the gooseberry, are great additions to the landscape. The currant especially, for two reasons I can think of right off the top of my head. One, the currant isn't quite as vigorous as the gooseberry and, while it requires regular pruning, will not become a scary thicket of prickly canes like its more rugged relative if you forget to prune for a year or so. Second, come mid-June, brilliant strands of glistening red berries will begin peeking out from within the dark green foliage. Once they ripen, the sweet-tart, juicy explosion

of each little berry will have you feverishly plucking the tiny gems from their stems. Oh, and I thought of a third! Currants are quite hardy in Zones 4 and 3, and some cultivars are hardy in Zone 2.

Gooseberries are, as I said, a little harder to handle, but well worth the effort. These beautifully veined, translucent berries are surprisingly delicious, and yes, gooseberry pie is as good as you remember it from grandma's kitchen. The bush grows in a fountain-like form, spreading with root suckers, but can also be trained as a standard (currants can be trained this way too). It can get out of hand if not pruned every year, so be aggressive and don't hold back with this one. Look for red-fruited varieties like 'Hinomakki Red' and 'Pixwell', and near-spineless varieties like 'Captivator' and 'Pax' (also red-fruited).

Fig
Ficus carica

This is one of those ancient fruits that has slipped out of the realm of the home garden. If your only experience with figs is the super-sweet puree inside little square cookies, you're in for a real treat. A fresh fig is earthy, floral, sweet, and absolutely delicious. Top half a fresh fig with bleu cheese and you'll wonder how you ever lived without them.

Thankfully for landscaping enthusiasts like us, figs grow on unusual, airy trees with unique gray-green leaves. Look for new dwarf or semi-dwarf varieties

MALJALEN/SHUTTERSTOCK

to fit into your landscape and ensure you can reach all the fruit. Larger varieties grow quite tall and produce lots of treats for birds, being far out of your reach.

Fig trees need a lot of sun to flower, and they enjoy heat through most of the season. In fact, you'll never actually see them flower, because the flowers are inside of what we think of as the fruit. Figs are very unique in this way, and some species require a specific wasp to pollinate the flowers. Thankfully, the common fig, which is most readily available in numerous cultivars, is parthenocarpic, meaning it doesn't need to be pollinated. Most are hardy in Zone 7 and can be grown as a tree or in a multistem bush form. If you live in a cooler region, try a dwarf fig in a container and bring it inside for the cold months, keeping it cool but above 20 degrees F during its dormancy. Placing it back outside as the temperatures warm in the spring should do the trick.

Grapes
Vitis spp.

Long-considered to be grown only on vast hillsides in wine-country, grapes have become a prized landscape plant in many home gardens. Whether for making wine or eating fresh, grapes definitely have a "wow factor" when grown at home. It's exciting to watch the miniscule flowers give way to tiny green berries, then mature into juicy clusters. If you grow grapes on an arbor, archway, or trellis, the clusters will literally hang before your eyes, taunting you with temptation until the time is right to harvest. Even varieties intended for wine are great for snacking. They have unique flavors all their own that are exciting to taste fresh.

There are wine industries popping up in regions you may not expect, so if you live in the North, Midwest, or Deep South you can grow grapes in your yard just as well as your gardening

GYUSZKOFOTO/SHUTTERSTOCK

friends in classic grape-growing areas. Be sure to find varieties that are suited to your climate.

Grapes can do a great job of disguising a fence or softening a garage wall. A garden obelisk or other free-standing trellis will also train the vine into a lovely form. If you train it as a weeping standard, visitors to your garden will be impressed by the stately grape.

Grapes need pruning every year to be productive, and severe pruning at that. They need deep, well-drained soil, but it doesn't have to be the greatest-quality soil. You'll want to avoid too much nitrogen because that can lead to too much foliage at the expense of fruit.

Hardy Kiwi
Actinidia kolomikta, Actinidia arguta

Hardy kiwi is one of the most talked about plants for northern gardens these days. If you're looking for a unique specimen (or two, as you'll discover) to wow your friends and produce piles of tasty fruit, this is the plant for you. Hardy kiwi, also known as hardy kiwifruit, kiwiberry, or Arctic kiwi, is different from the big, brown, fuzzy kiwifruit we know from New Zealand. The hardy kiwi produces grape-sized, smooth fruit on a

RUSSAL/SHUTTERSTOCK

perennial vine hardy in Zone 3. And this vine is vigorous. It can grow up to twenty feet a year and needs a sturdy trellis or structure to support all that growth. It's a very handy plant to soften a large deck or pergola.

The foliage is dense and lush, and some varieties have red stems or variegated leaves to add even more intrigue. In the spring, the vines will produce a plethora of little white/yellow flowers that have a sweet, tropical scent. In order for those flowers to become tasty fruits, you'll need to have both male and female plants. Usually one male plant will suffice to provide pollen for up to eight female plants. Even with both male and female plants, you'll have to be patient with the hardy kiwi. It generally takes a few years for the plants to start flowering, and a spring frost can sometimes kill the flowers, meaning a year without fruit. In those years, enjoy the vine for its foliage and ensure your anxious friends that once it does produce fruit, there'll be plenty to go around.

Peach, plum, apricot, and cherry
Prunus spp.

Trees and shrubs in the *Prunus* family are some of the most graceful and attractive trees available. Ornamental *Prunus* like flowering almond and weeping cherry are prized for their spectacular blooms in the early spring. The unique thing about *Prunus* is the flowers bloom before any leaves appear, so you'll have this beautiful tree covered with nothing but flowers for a few

weeks each year. Another great thing about *Prunus* is that the fruiting varieties are just as lovely as the ornamental varieties. And the flowers have a sweet fragrance that smells lightly of the fruits they'll become.

All *Prunus* trees bloom early in the spring—very early. In cooler regions this can be a challenge. In some years, the flowers will bloom and then be damaged by frost, meaning few or no fruit that year. But in the years that spring is gentle and mild, the trees will be covered with delicious fruit. Look for varieties that are hardy in your area. Most are hardy to Zone 5, but you'll find several that work in Zone 4. For cooler regions, try 'Alderman' and 'Superior' plum, 'Moongold' and 'Sungold' apricot, and 'North Star', 'Meteor', and 'Mesabi' cherries. These are just a few suggestions, but there are plenty of varieties out there that will work for your area. One important factor to keep in mind, most *Prunus* trees require at least two different varieties to ensure pollination, except for the tart cherries, which are generally self-fruitful.

Pears
Pyrus spp.

Pear trees are majestic, graceful, long-lived trees that look lovely in a landscape. There are varieties that can grow in almost any region, from Florida to Arizona, Maine to Washington, and just about everywhere in between. Classic grocery store varieties such as 'Bosc' and 'Bartlett' require a mild climate, but cold-hardy selections like 'Gourmet,' 'Luscious', 'Summercrisp', and 'Ure' will suit most northern gardeners. The fruit on cold-region trees is generally smaller, but has very good flavor.

Pear trees tend to be very productive, as long as they have adequate pollination. Most pear varieties require cross-pollination from another variety to produce a full crop. Unlike apples (another fruit that requires cross-pollination), which would likely produce a full crop with only one tree due to the fact that ornamental crab apple trees are prevalent in many areas, pears are much less common. The

likelihood of another pear tree within range of bees and other pollinators is probably small for most home growers. However, some pear trees will produce a little fruit all on their own, which might be sufficient, because in general pear trees are rather large. Traditionally a pear tree can grow taller than twenty-five feet, making it tricky to harvest and prune. Some are now grown on dwarfing rootstocks or semi-dwarfing rootstocks, making them smaller and better suited to home gardens. When buying a tree, be sure to find out about this, and do some research to make sure the variety is hardy in your area.

You'll want to be sure to pick up any dropped fruit throughout the season since rotting fruit on the ground attracts wasps and promotes disease. Pear trees are known to have trouble with fire blight, a bacterial disease that can kill the tree. There are many resistant varieties available, but resistant doesn't mean immune, so proper pruning, sanitation, and care are important to keep your pear tree healthy, beautiful, and productive for many years to come.

Pomegranate
Punica granatum
Pomegranate is a highly ornamental fruit plant best suited to landscapes in warm, sunny, dry regions. This fruit, whose ancient appeal has made it a prominent symbol in countless cultures throughout history, has great value as a

NIR DAROM/SHUTTERSTOCK

versatile landscape plant as well. Pomegranate grows naturally as a rounded shrub, filling out through the production of many suckers. It can be grown as a specimen, as a hedge, or even trained as an attractive, small tree if one stem is chosen as the trunk and suckers are removed regularly. Even when grown as a shrub, suckers should be thinned to prevent too dense a plant.

The real excitement comes when this easy-to-grow plant flowers and fruits. The flowers are bright red, last quite a long time, and attract hummingbirds. The flowers are replaced by equally spectacular fruits, creating the effect of ornaments on a Christmas tree. The hefty, leathery fruits are an exquisite contrast to the narrow, shiny, dark green leaves.

Pomegranate is generally self-fertile, but fruit set will be greater with two or more cultivars.

Plenty of sun is also needed for good fruit set, and it'll take a couple of years to get good fruit set, so be patient. And in the first couple of years, fruit drop may be significant, but don't despair. Let this plant grow up a little and it'll likely produce fruit for fifteen or twenty years!

Raspberry
Rubus spp.
Raspberries have a notoriously bad reputation in the garden. We love them for their sweet berries, but for all their deliciousness they have one particular characteristic that puts them into the "I'd love to grow them but. . ." category: that characteristic is underground runners. See, while it's distracting you with the promise of delicious fruit, this mischievous plant is sending aggressive roots out across the garden with the intent to conquer. One seemingly innocent plant will, the following spring, send up shoots several feet away from the original, like little soldiers ready to fight for their rights to the land. And fight they will. Try to dig these out and you'll discover a massive network of runners that will easily root

and become plants, even the smallest broken piece. To reign them in you need to eradicate every bit of those runners.

Wait, don't stop reading. There is hope. You don't have to be a victim of your raspberries. You can conquer, or at least subdue, this warrior of the garden. Try planting raspberries in containers and sinking those in the garden. Or build a raised bed with a deep lining of landscape fabric that comes all the way up to the top edge of the soil. Chances are the runners won't be able to poke through the fabric. Most importantly, you simply need to give them the attention they're pining for: prune and thin the plants regularly. By regularly I mean every year and every time you see a shoot coming up where you don't want it. You'll show that raspberry who is the ruler of your garden and be rewarded with sweet, juicy berries for weeks each year.

Strawberry
Fragaria spp.
A freshly picked strawberry on a sunny day is the flavor of summer. Different types of strawberries have very different growth habits, so depending on how you want to grow the plant, be sure you know what type you're getting. June-bearing strawberries send out a lot of runners to spread, and I mean *a lot*. These runners create little daughter plants at the ends, which root and eventually send out runners of their own. This

means strawberries can spread quickly, which is good if you have an empty space you want to fill with a ground cover. But they can grow too much for their own good and actually choke themselves out. Control them by directing runners to areas you want new plants to root. Simply move the runner where you want it, and gently press the end of it into the ground. Excess runners can be clipped off at the base of the mother plant, and daughter plants potted and given to friends. Thin the bed by pulling out older plants at the end of the season.

Day-neutral or ever-bearing types don't runner as much, putting more of their energy into producing fruit. They'll usually produce two crops, one in the spring and one in the late summer. These are generally not as cold-hardy, so options will be limited in cooler regions.

Alpine strawberries are little wonders of the landscape, especially in northern regions. These native plants are smaller than commercial varieties, both the plant and the fruit. What they're lacking in size, however, they make up for in flavor. The tiny berries, about

the size of a thumbnail, pack an intense, aromatic flavor into a very small package. Alpine strawberries are naturally shade tolerant, their native habitat being the understory and edges of woodlands. Plant these little beauties on shady borders, under trees or shrubs. They don't spread like the June-bearers, so they'll be easy to control.

All strawberries look great combined with other plants. June-bearers create a nice understory for tall plants like eggplants and tomatoes and will generally be done flowering and fruiting by the time the other plants start shading them out. At that point the strawberries' glossy green foliage creates a lovely carpet of green under taller plants. The diminutive alpine strawberry pairs well with small-scale plants like leaf lettuces, dwarf greens, and non-aggressive ornamentals like impatiens or lobelia.

HERBS

I love herbs, not only for their ability to liven up recipes, but for the fact that, as plants, they're generally very easygoing. Plant oregano or sage in the garden and you can be pretty sure you won't have to bother with it much throughout the season. And happily, the more you clip from them the more they produce—well, within reason, anyway. Full sun is best for most herbs, since it will make them vigorous and flavorful.

I don't have to elaborate on how most of these herbs are valued in cooking, but a few might be unfamiliar. Fresh herbs add so much more zip to recipes than their dried counterparts, so it is a real treat to have access to so much flavorful goodness during the season. Most herbs grow well in containers, so if you have cold, harsh winters, you can bring them inside, give them some good light, and enjoy them all year long.

I use a lot of herbs in my landscape . . . and I mean a lot. They're great fillers, border plants and ground covers. Most are quite easy to grow, with few pest problems. In fact many herbs are believed to help keep pests away from the garden due to their volatile oils. Harvest herbs early and often to promote new growth and to get the most flavorful, young cuttings. Generally herbs taste their best before flower initiation, but it's worth it at some point in the season to let them flower. When they do, their blooms attract an amazing number of pollinators and other beneficial insects. The flowers of most herbs are nice to harvest also and can be sprinkled in salads or used in cooking for a light herb flavor.

Basil
Basilicum spp.
Ah, basil. No summer garden should be without it. This sun-loving, Mediterranean herb is the perfect partner to tomatoes in the kitchen and in the garden. It is often said that basil

FOODPICTURES/SHUTTERSTOCK

planted around tomato plants can promote the health, vigor, and flavor of the tomatoes. It's definitely worth a try because basil also looks fantastic planted with tomatoes. Something about that smooth, shiny leaf contrasts nicely with the more rugged foliage of the tomato.

Of course, basil is a great landscape plant for other areas of the garden too. Look for purple, burgundy, and variegated varieties for an extra punch of color. These varieties aren't always as sweet as traditional basil, but often have exciting spicy hints or citrus flavors that perk up any recipe. A variegated variety, 'Pesto Perpetuo' has creamy white leaf margins and generally will not flower. Harvest all other basils frequently to prevent flowering, which will cause flavor and production to decline. To delay flowering, it's necessary to clip the main stem above a lower level of leaves. The plant will branch out from that node and give you more

savory basil to use throughout the season.

For something completely different, try growing globe basil, often called 'Spicy Globe' or 'Greek' basil. These varieties have very small leaves, only about ¼ to ½ inch long, and grow naturally into a round shrub shape, about eight to twelve inches in diameter. Globe basil has a slightly spicy flavor, making it great for sprinkling on pizza, pasta, and salads. Planted in containers or along a path in a formal setting, these little green orbs need hardly any attention to keep them looking great. Clip small sprigs often to keep the shape tidy and to prevent flowering.

Chervil
Anthriscus cerefolium
Chervil is not widely known or grown in gardens. It's a relative of parsley and most resembles the flat-leaf varieties, but has a lighter texture in the garden due to its finely cut, fringy

SUNDEBO/SHUTTERSTOCK

leaves. Unlike most herbs, this one actually prefers some shade, because it bolts quickly in the heat of summer. This small, delicate plant is elegant along borders and works well interplanted with lettuces, broccoli, radishes, and beets. The pale green color and airy texture provide contrast to low-growing colorful flowers.

Chervil has a delicate parsley flavor with a hint of anise. Use it in mixed green salads for a little extra flavor. Harvest the outer stems and leaves throughout the season. Continued harvest will encourage new growth and help delay bolting. The plant will turn purple-bronze later in the season, and at this point, keep it for its color. The flavor declines once it turns color.

Chives
Allium spp.
Chives are taken for granted in the garden. If a person grows any number of herbs, most likely chives are there. They're snipped to sprinkle onto the occasional baked potato, but sadly they're often neglected, tucked in the garden somewhere inconspicuous, their virtues reduced to little but occasional utility. This is unfortunate, because the chive plant is a perky, easygoing plant that does wonders in the garden while asking nothing special from the gardener. The plant flourishes just about anywhere (though it prefers sun), in any soil, and will come back year after year even in the coldest regions. It's

VOLKER RAUCH/SHUTTERSTOCK

one of the earliest to appear in spring and will grow happily through the first couple of frosts of autumn. Chives are generally pest-free and are even known to deter some pests in the garden. They are easy to start from seed and seem to love the disturbance of being divided. Chives will self-seed readily, so simply trim off the purple flowers before they go to seed. The flowers can be crumbled apart and used to add a splash of color to salads or any other dish needing a hint of light onion flavor.

All this and they're good looking, too! Chives' straight, rush-like leaves add a grassy touch to the landscape, contrasting well with broad-leaf plants. Plant chives with tomatoes, carrots, cabbage-family plants and even apple trees to help ward off pests. Chives are perfectly at home with ornamentals, adding a touch of green in among all that color.

Don't stop at traditional onion chives. Garlic chives have a distinct flat leaf and a beautiful white starburst flower. These will go wild if left to seed, so cut those flower stalks out and use them in the kitchen. Garlic chives have a lovely, light garlic flavor and come in handy when you've discovered you have no garlic in the pantry. Also look for dwarf chives and varieties of German chives for something a little different in the landscape. All are edible and have their own light onion flavor.

Dill
Anethum graveolens
Dill in the landscape means pickles and pollinators. Yes, not only is dill the quintessential ingredient in one of the easiest preserved veggies, it is also one of the very best at attracting pollinators and other beneficial insects to the garden. This tall, airy herb gives off a heavenly scent on hot summer days, and

all those insects can't pass up a sip of its nectar. While they're in the neighborhood, they're bound to visit other plants and feast on a pest or two.

Dill is a star as a background plant, especially the larger varieties that grow to four or five feet tall. Its pale green hue and feathery texture provide the perfect foil to coarser textured, colorful ornamentals. It works well surrounded by sturdy perennials that will help support it later in the season when it gets a bit too tall for its own strength.

Against all advice to the contrary, I like to leave dill in the garden through the fall when it takes on a rich copper color. Of course at this point, the lacy flower heads have gone to seed and are happily scattering them all over the garden. This becomes a problem in the spring when all these seeds germinate and I find mini dill plants in places I never would have expected they could travel to. But it's worth it for the color and height it brings to the garden as the summer days are fading into fall.

Lavender
Lavandula spp.
The sweet, floral scent of lavender floating on the warm summer air can transport a person to faraway places in an instant. There's something intrinsically powerful about lavender, and generally you either love it or hate it. If you're one of those people who love this seductive herb, then you will likely want to plant a lot of it.

AUTHOR PHOTO

Not only for its heady fragrance, but for the silvery green foliage and airy spikes of flowers. Those of us in the North, if we want our lavender to overwinter, are limited to a few hardy English varieties like 'Munstead' and 'Hidcote', which still need a bit of pampering to make it through the winter. Thankfully for us Northerners, it is the English lavenders that have the classic scent and are generally preferred in cooking. There's a visual subtlety about English lavender that makes it all the more surprising when a slight brush of the hand releases that intoxicating aroma. In warmer climates, French and Spanish lavenders offer showier options.

Lavender tends to grow a little taller than most border plants, yet that's where I like to use it so I'm able brush past and smell it when I'm walking through or working in the garden. The fine-leaved, silvery foliage topped by tall, slender flower spikes has a distinct appearance in the landscape. For an airy, cottage garden look, plant it in front of tall ornamentals like nicotiana and cleome (both non-edible). Lavender, like many aromatic herbs, is believed to help repel insect pests, specifically those that attack plants in the cabbage family. Thankfully, it looks great planted with the coarse, fleshy cabbage relatives.

Mint
Mentha spp.
Mint is one of those plants we love to hate . . . or hate to love. It's a great herb to have in the garden for its aroma and for all the ways it's used in drinks, desserts, salads, and cooking. But this aggressive grower has caused many a gardener many a headache in attempts to eradicate it after it has spread far beyond its intended boundaries. Mint of nearly all varieties grows quickly and propagates through runners that spread far and wide.

It will cheerfully choke out any other plants in its vicinity, but somehow it manages to hold our affection because of its sweet, candy-and-chewing-gum appeal. It's also a good-looking plant, and the different varieties lend themselves well to the landscape.

Thankfully, you can grow your mint and control it, too, by using containers. Keep some in a pot on the patio, planted with a few colorful ornamentals for easy access. Or if you want mint in your garden, simply plant it in a plastic container with drainage holes and sink the whole thing in the ground. The mint will have a harder time spreading thanks to the barrier the container provides. Place a mesh screen over the drainage holes, just in case any sneaky roots try to find their way out the bottom. Peppermint has a more trailing habit than spearmint and will root if a stem comes in contact with the soil. So be careful, even with containerized plants, to trim them back often to keep this from happening. For a little extra height in the garden, place a container of mint (with a saucer under it) right on the ground in the middle of the other plants.

Oregano
Origanum vulgare
Fresh oregano has the aroma of rustic stone kitchens in the Italian countryside. The flavor it lends to food is one of those things that make us close our eyes in delight at the first bite. Growing oregano in your landscape will give you plenty

AUTHOR PHOTO

to use fresh and to freeze or dry for use in the winter.

This humble plant is soft green with small, oval or near-heart-shaped leaves. Some varieties have smooth leaves, others slightly fuzzy. It hugs the ground when young, but grows up into a mounded form twelve to twenty-four inches tall. It sends out runners to help it spread, which look lovely cascading over the edges of a container filled with veggies and flowers. It's a perfect border plant or small-space groundcover, spreading gently and easily, controlled by simply harvesting often for use in the kitchen. Oregano pairs nicely with low-growing, colorful annuals like petunias and alyssum.

Greek oregano (*Origanium vulgare hirtum*) is considered to have the best flavor for cooking, but the common oregano has pleasant flavor, too, and is hardier—a perennial in Zone 5 but able to survive cooler regions with snow or mulch cover. This herb will become woody over time, so be sure to harvest regularly, prune in the spring, and divide every couple of years.

Parsley
Petroselinum hortense
Parsley is a great filler, border, and general do-gooder in the landscape. Flat-leaf and curly varieties are both welcome additions for their use in the kitchen and their distinct appearances. Flat-leaf varieties tend to be a little taller and airier, and the deep green, shiny leaves certainly catch the eye. Curly parsley has a deep, ruffled green that fills in more densely along borders or at the base of tall plants like tomatoes or okra. Try interplanting parsley with similar-sized flowering plants, like violas. The way the flowers grow up through the parsley and peek their colorful heads through that foliage is delightful! The same could be said for petunias or calibrachoa (both non-edible) and other light-textured ornamentals.

Parsley is thought to have some pest-resistant qualities and may help repel asparagus beetles

KLETR/SHUTTERSTOCK

and some tomato pests. When left to flower, it attracts syrphid flies and parasitic wasps, both good guys in the garden. A real treat parsley brings to the garden is black swallowtail butterfly caterpillars. I have found lots of these striped wonders munching on my parsley, and when I do I am happy to sacrifice a little parsley for these beauties. Parsley is one of their favorite foods, along with dill and fennel.

Sage
Salvia officinalis

Sage is such a unique-looking plant, and with all the varieties of color and flavor the possibilities for it in the landscape are many. Garden sage, also known as common sage, is the classic for cooking. Its elliptical leaves have a soft texture that is unlike any other plant I know. This velvety, mounding plant has an ethereal silver-green color, making it a good companion to brightly colored plants and flowers. Try pairing it with colorful chard or calendula.

Garden sage is the hardiest of the many varieties available, generally a perennial in Zone 3.

If you can find them, colored varieties add an interesting touch to the garden. Look for purple, tricolor, and golden sages to spice up the landscape and your table—they have virtually the same flavor as garden sage, but may not be quite as hardy.

Plant sage at the base of tomatoes to conceal bare stems. Try planting sage with cabbage family or carrot plants to help repel certain pests. Interplanting with strawberries may help to prevent insect pests while creating visual contrast. When sage flowers, spikes of pale lavender flowers hover above the airy plant and attract all kinds of beneficial insects. The flowers are lovely used in bouquets, both fresh and dried.

After over-wintering for a couple of years, sage will start to get woody and sparse. This might be slowed if you harvest often during the season and prune out the oldest, woodiest stems in early spring. Chances are, sage will need to be replaced every three to four years to keep it full and looking good. Garden sage and colored varieties are readily available in garden centers and easy to start from seed (indoors, late winter).

Summer savory
Satureja hortensis

Summer savory doesn't show up in gardens a whole lot these days. This is one of those "herbs of old" that few people know what to do with in the kitchen anymore. Once prized for its medicinal qualities and

NORALUCA013/SHUTTERSTOCK

distinct thyme-dill-mint-pepper flavor, summer savory has fallen into the shadows of basil and oregano, herbs that have become superstars in almost every garden. But this herb, a classic ingredient in "herbs de Provence," has a wonderful flavor that livens up beans, sauteed mushrooms, roasted vegetables, meats, and fish.

Summer savory is a nice little plant, and that alone begs inclusion in any landscape. This low-growing, bushy annual is easy to start from seed and will self-seed for next season. The plant has the look of a miniature shrub. It is open and airy, with small, purple-tinged leaves and thin stems that become woody later in the season. In mid-summer tiny purple flowers will dot the plant and welcome a multitude of bees and other pollinators. In fact, savory has a history of being a great plant to grow near beehives, producing a lightly herbal honey. This is one of those long-lost herbs that deserve a renaissance in the garden.

Thyme
Thymus vulgaris

Thyme is a staple in any kitchen garden. This diminutive plant is easy to grow and takes on a natural mounded, gently spreading form. Garden or common thyme is most readily available in garden centers and generally has the best flavor for cooking. You might see French and English thyme, and these are varieties of common thyme. Countless other varieties can be found with citrus scents, variegation, low-growing, or trailing habits. These are also edible and add variety to the landscape. Remember, none will quite have that classic, intense thyme flavor, so you may want to pop in a few garden thyme plants for that.

Garden thyme is a sweet little plant. When young, it has soft, green stems with tiny leaves. It becomes woody over time, but regular harvesting and light pruning will help keep it from getting too woody. Woodier stems tend not to put out as much new growth, so keep it nicely pruned and shaped for best production. Most varieties are hardy in Zone 5, but will likely survive winter

FEDOR KONDRATENKO/SHUTTERSTOCK

in Zone 4 with a good snow cover or mulch.

Thyme looks nice as a border plant and works well interplanted with other small-scale plants like alyssum or creeping phlox. It only grows to about a foot tall, so keep that in mind when choosing placement and companions. It will be happiest in full sun and will reward you with dense, tiny green foliage and delicious flavor.

EDIBLE FLOWERS

I must add a disclaimer here that not all flowers are edible, and before you consume any flower you must be absolutely sure you know that it is indeed an edible variety. Some flowers are very poisonous. Some others not quite so, but will probably make you ill if you eat them. Please be sure you know the plant before you eat it.

In the descriptions here I've noted parts of the plants that are most palatable. Other parts may be edible, but I cannot say for sure that they will taste good or that they are completely safe to eat. Relatives of the plants mentioned here are not necessarily edible. If you plan to venture into the world of foraging and the like, please find a reputable guidebook to keep you informed and safe.

Bachelor button
Centaurea cyanus
I love easygoing plants that appear cheerful in any

conditions, and bachelor button is one of those plants. You may have seen this unassuming plant along the edges of a country road and know it as cornflower. This heritage goes to show that bachelor button doesn't require the best growing conditions. Yes, this plant can be considered a weed and may become invasive in some areas. But in climates that freeze during the winter, this isn't so much of a problem. Bachelor button may self-seed, but I've never had it do so very successfully—just a few plants here and there.

Bachelor button has small, 1 ½-inch blue flowers that bobble atop tall, fine, gray-green stems. You may find purple and pink varieties, but blue is my favorite since it's rare to find a good blue for the garden. The plant is very upright in nature, and it actually amazes me sometimes that it can hold itself up, as slender as it is. The overall cool color and light texture of bachelor button makes it a good contrast to coarser plants like chard and tomatoes, and of course it looks great paired with all kinds of herbs. It adds a cottage-like feel to the garden when planted in masses and attracts bees and many other beneficial insects. It's perfect for use as a cut flower and retains its color when dried.

Bachelor button's blue flowers are edible, contributing a delicate spicy-sweet flavor to salads and a splash of color atop steamed greens. The petals can also be used dried in teas.

Bee balm/Monarda
Monarda didyma, Monarda fistulosa
This colorful member of the mint family is a mainstay in the garden, if for no other reason than its ability to attract pollinators. But there are many other reasons to give this striking plant a prominent place in your landscape. Monarda is a tall, colorful perennial that gives structure and height to the landscape. It's nice to know it'll be back year after year as a foundation to the rest of the garden. Monarda is a hardy perennial, native to many parts of the United States. There are many improved cultivars available with bright and varied bloom colors and resistance to powdery mildew. Most cultivars maintain hardiness in Zone 4.

The flowers and leaves can be used in cooking, salads, teas, and medicinal applications. The plant has a lovely minty-bergamot scent that insects and hummingbirds can't resist. Cut a few bright, starburst-shaped flowers to use in bouquets with herbs and other edible flowers for a unique conversation piece.

Borage
Borago officinalis
I grew borage for the first time a couple of years ago and was utterly amazed by the number of bees this unique plant attracts. The first year I planted a couple of large masses of borage. Since then I've spread it out, planting masses of it here and there where I need a coarse textured, mid-height flowering plant in the garden.

Borage has a coarse texture due to its thick stems, fleshy leaves, and dense fuzz over the entire plant, except the flower petals. These hairs are generally soft but become a bit prickly and irritating with age. Gloves are a good idea when working with borage if you're a sensitive soul. This fuzz gives borage an ethereal appearance that makes it striking in the garden and lends it an unexpected lightness. The small delicate flowers that hover atop the plant add to this effect. The flowers are a cool blue color, almost electric, and this electricity is like a magnet for bees. They hover about the plant all season long.

Borage is edible, having a light cucumber flavor. Yet, because of the fuzzy texture of the leaves, most people prefer to use only the flowers. They're lovely as a garnish on soups and serve to brighten up a summer salad.

Calendula
Calendula officinalis
Another cheery addition to the landscape is calendula, sometimes known as pot

marigold, even though it is not a marigold at all. Calendula will add some of the most vibrant color to the landscape, in bright, clean yellows, oranges, reds, and all variants of those. The entire plant has a distinct fragrance, especially on a hot day. This is one of the easiest flowers to grow, since it will pop up from seed in almost any conditions. Planted in masses, calendula will brighten up any garden, looking good with chard, tomatoes, herbs . . . pretty much anywhere you need a splash of color.

My love of calendula fades a little when it comes time to start dead-heading. Calendula flowers profusely, and all those bright flowers are bound to go to seed, and when they do, boy, are they obvious. The cheery flowers are replaced by big, gnarly seed-heads that, when ripe, disperse their large, sickle-shaped seeds all over. The calendula bed goes from a cheery place in the garden to a slightly scary, brown eyesore. This is easily prevented by dead-heading, but you must do it early and regularly. Otherwise the task becomes daunting. Keep on top of it though, and you'll be rewarded with bright blooms all season, right on into the chilly days of autumn.

The petals of the flower are edible, as are the leaves, though they don't have the best flavor. A few in a mild green salad can add a punch of flavor though. The petals are like colorful confetti when mixed into a salad and add a touch of bitterness. The pigment in calendula petals

adds gold color to rice and other dishes, giving this plant the nickname "poor man's saffron." Calendula is known to have many medicinal properties as well.

Nasturtium
Tropaeolum spp.
Nasturtium: the classic edible flower. This plant had a heyday sometime in the 1980s when suddenly nasturtium flowers were the wild and creative things to put in a salad. The mere thought of being able to eat a flower blew us away. Well, the fervor has faded, and finding flowers in your salad is no longer such a groundbreaking concept. But that hasn't changed the fact that nasturtium is an interesting plant. There's nothing else quite like it in terms of form, leaf shape, flower shape, and color. Some varieties grow in a mound and remain well-behaved, while some trail on to the ends of the earth, making them perfect for trellises, fences, even mailbox posts. Its saucer-shaped leaves are definitely unique, surpassed

only by its intensely bright flowers. The deep nectar tubes on the flowers make them attractive to insects. There are countless varieties in a rainbow of colors, but my favorites are variegates with speckled and striped white or pale green patches on the leaves and paler flower colors. The variegation helps to break up the green in the garden and give the eye something to stop and ponder.

Nasturtium is widely thought to be a good companion plant, with a propensity to repel squash bugs, cucumber beetles, and several brassica pests. I've interplanted them with my zucchini, but still got squash bugs, so I'm not so sure about their repellant nature. But they always have a place in my garden for their interesting appearance, ability to quickly fill a void, and profusion of edible flowers. Plant them around tomatoes for a wave of color beneath the tall stems. Nasturtium looks great falling over the edges of a retaining wall or container.

Pansy and viola
Viola spp.
These sweet little plants are great to tuck in here and there where you need to fill space along borders, between lettuces and small herbs. One of my favorite plant combinations is violas and parsley. By alternating them in a border or small bed, the flowers intermingle with the parsley leaves, peeking out here and there, adding a splash of color to the green parsley. The

same effect is achieved with chervil or cilantro.

Viola has smaller flowers than the showy pansy. I like the understated nature of the viola. Pansies tend to have too much flower for the size of the plant, and the flowers seem to look a bit floppy. Both are lovely though and have edible flowers that brighten everything from salads to quiches, and sparkle atop cakes and candies when coated with sugar.

Violas are easy to grow and are available at garden centers in a wide range of colors. They like cool temperatures and can tolerate a touch of shade, so plant them along with your lettuces and other greens in a cooler spot in the garden. They'll fill in the gaps as you harvest greens and small root veggies like radishes. Their flowering may slow in the heat of the summer but will pick right up again as autumn sets in.

Signet marigold
Tagetes tenuifolia
If I could choose only one edible flower to grow in my landscape it would be the signet marigold, sometimes known as gem marigold. These little beauties are unlike any marigolds you've seen before. The flowers are tiny for a marigold (only about ¾ inch in diameter), and they cover a small (twelve- to fourteen-inch) mound of lacy, green foliage. These marigolds are easy to start from seed (which will be necessary until they get popular enough to start popping up in garden centers) and grow quickly into a naturally rounded shape.

I'm generally not a big marigold fan, primarily due to their ubiquity in the garden. But these little guys always find a place in my landscape. Why are signet marigolds so great, you ask? Well, I appreciate them most for their cheery colors that are like a bright smile in the midst of a lot of green. But they're not overly showy like their African and French cousins. The size of their blooms better fits the scale of the foliage. The cute, compact round shape of the plant is unique for a marigold and generally garners lots of interest from passers-by. Their

low stature makes them perfect for borders or under taller plants (think tomatoes). In fact they do well with a bit of light shade from larger plants, because in the heat of the summer they'll get a little tired and bloom will slow. Flowering will pick back up in the fall, however. Some gardeners cut them close to the ground during the peak heat of summer, and wait for cooler days when the plants will regenerate.

The petals of this marigold are edible and have a light citrus-tarragon flavor, perfect to brighten up a green salad.

ORNAMENTALS

Alyssum
Lobularia maritima
Alyssum is the ornamental annual to choose if you're looking to attract insects to the garden. Try interplanting alyssum with thyme, oregano, and other small-stature herbs: the tiny scale of the leaves and the flowers make them perfect partners on borders. Alyssum is definitely a light textured, delicate plant and flowers in equally delicate shades of purple, pink, and white. It's easy to grow, spreads to form

a carpet of delicate color, and many varieties have a delicious scent. Alyssum works well in containers, cascading gently over the edges. Plant it in a container with mixed greens—kale, lettuce, and mizuna mustard—to add a breath of lightness to the mix.

Cosmos
Cosmos spp.

Cosmos always makes me smile. I'm a sucker for its big, bright flowers with yellow centers. It looks like it's always feeling happy: the way those flowers bob around in the lightest breeze above all that fringy foliage . . . it's like they're always dancing. And for that cosmos makes me smile. Therefore, I find a spot for this cheery annual in my garden every year. Thankfully there's a lot of variety in cosmos, so I never feel as if I'm planting the same old thing. You'll find cosmos varieties that grow only a foot or so tall, and others that tower at four or five feet. Foliage ranges from delicate and threadlike to slightly broader and more truly leaf-like. Flowers might

be very simple and aster-esque, sea shell-shaped, or full and fringy. No matter the variety, the colorful, broad, open flowers are welcoming to all kinds of garden-friendly insects.

Echinacea
Echinacea spp.

There's a species of echinacea native to just about every place in the United States, making it a natural choice for gardens everywhere. The cultivated and improved varieties take this plant beyond its humble purple and copper flowered origins to the realm of sunset oranges, fire engine reds, and grassy greens. In some varieties, the rugged coneflowers at the center have been coaxed into ray flowers, creating a bloom that is a bizarre, two-tiered extravaganza of floriforousness.

Borrowed from the prairie, echinacea is a valuable food source for insects and birds alike. While you may not want an

excess of birds in your garden, the little songbirds that I've occasionally seen perched on my coneflower have done no harm. They don't seem to have much interest until winter, when the seed heads are bursting with flavor. Hold off on cutting these back till spring to enjoy the appearance of the delicate, dark stems and seed-heads against the pale winter sky.

Echinacea is known to have medicinal properties and is used in teas and remedies. I don't consider it an edible, however, because the flowers are not recommended for fresh eating and are generally only used when dried.

Rudbeckia
Rudbeckia spp.

A classic in perennial gardens, rudbeckia (black-eyed susan) is a great addition to a garden full of edibles. Depending on where you live, you may find both annual and perennial rudbeckia species.

AUTHOR PHOTO

I love the perennial rudbeckia for its staying power in the garden. It's one of those plants I can rely on year after year to provide structure and foundation for all the annual veggies I plant around it. The golden flowers appear in midsummer and persist through the cool days of autumn. When the petals finally fall, the plant is left with deep brown seed heads that are a delight to winter birds. Definitely don't cut these back until early spring. Not only do they give the birds a little midwinter snack, but they give form and interest to the garden during the off-season. On snowy days, the seed-heads look as if they're wearing little white caps. The body of the plant catches the snow and holds it close to the ground, helping to protect the roots from subzero temperatures.

Yarrow
Achillea millefolia
Yarrow has become my number-one favorite ornamental plant in the landscape. This hardy perennial comes back bigger and better every year. I've moved and divided it every year for four years, and each time it seems grateful for the attention. Once yarrow blooms there is rarely a moment it isn't being visited by some type of insect, be it a wild bee, lady beetle, parasitic wasp, or syrphid fly. Yarrow's light, ferny texture provides a good contrast to coarser textured plants. Many cultivars are available with a rainbow of flower colors from white and

palest yellow to deep burgundy. Spent flowers turn a brown tinge and aren't very attractive, so I cut them often before they brown and use the flower umbels in bouquets.

Zinnia
Zinnia spp.
Zinnia is a classic garden annual and one of my favorites. The bright, pure colors of zinnia are a delightful addition to the landscape and make for exquisite cut flowers. Several zinnia varieties are available to the gardener and range in height from twelve to thirty-six inches tall. With this range of heights, zinnia can be placed in many different areas of the garden. I think zinnias look best when planted in large, multicolored masses. Plant taller varieties behind chard and kale; the bright colors of the flowers will contrast nicely with the deep greens

of the chard and kale leaves. Shorter varieties do well in the second tier of a border, behind lettuces, arugula, or the frilly-textured mizuna mustard. Zinnia shines when planted to break up large areas of green. Zinnia is notorious for powdery mildew late in the season, however, so look for resistant varieties.

appendix
selected plants for northern landscapes

VEGETABLES

Code	Plant	Botanical Name	Varieties of Note	Form	Texture	Landscape Uses	Width	Height	Notes
A/E	Artichoke	Cynara sp.	Imperial Star	Upright	Coarse	Height, texture	2–3'	3–6'	Choose a variety known to produce buds in the first year if you're in an area with a short growing season and harsh winters.
P/E	Asparagus	Asparagus officinalis	Jersey Knight, Purple Passion	Upright, spreading	Fine	Height	12"	3–4'	Best to buy 1-year-old crowns for planting. Many varieties perennial in cooler regions. Bed can last 15+ years. Slow to establish.
A/E	Bean	Phaseolus vulgaris	Rattlesnake, Scarlet Runner, Trionfo Violetto, Royal Burgundy	Climbing, upright	Medium	Trellis	6–10"	6–8'	Plant near decorative support or trellis. Plant along with a flowering vine (ex. Thunbergia, morning glory) for even more visual interest.
A/E	Broccoli raab/Rapini	Brassica rapa var. ruvo		Upright	Medium	Mass, border, beneficials	1–3"	12"	Produces small broccoli-like florets. Attractive, small yellow flowers attract beneficials.
A/E	Carrot	Daucus carota var. sativus	Purple Dragon, Scarlet Nantes, Danvers	Rosette	Fine	Mass, border, part shade	1–3"	12"	Feathery texture of greens contrasts well with coarser plants. Keep in mind void left after harvest.
A/E	Celery	Apium graveolens var. dulce	Cutting Celery, Red Venture	Upright	Coarse	Mass, part shade	6"	18"	New cutting varieties can be harvested all season. Stick-straight, upright form is unique and a nice foil for bushier companions.
A/E	Chard	Beta vulgaris var. cicla	Bright Lights Mix, Rainbow Mix, Neon Lights Mix, Magic Red, Golden Sunrise	Rosette	Coarse	Mass, border, container, part shade	12–15"	12"	Wide range of leaf and stem colors. Grows well in cool and hot temps. Generally will not bolt. Very few pest problems. Direct seed or transplant. Will tolerate light shade. Very easy to grow. Harvest throughout season.
A/E	Eggplant	Solanum melongena var. esculentum	Hansel, Gretel, Rotunda Bianca, Round Mauve, Pandora Striped Rose, Calliope, Biolette di Firenze, Ghostbuster, Casper	Upright	Medium to coarse	Specimen, texture	18–24"	18–22"	Smaller-fruited varieties rarely require support. Silvery foliage. Nice plant architecture.
P/E	Hops	Humulus lupulus	Cascade, Centennial, Mt. Hood	Climbing, spreading	Coarse	Trellis	5'	20–25'	Flowers not recommended for eating, but rather are used in brewing. Young shoots can be used like asparagus. Clip young shoots for eating before they become prickly. Vines die back in winter, and spread via underground rhizomes.
A/E	Kale	Brassica oleracea	Dinosaur, Lacinato, Tuscan, Red Russian, Redbor	Rosette	Coarse	Mass, border, part shade	16–18"	2–3'	Wide range of leaf colors, shapes, and textures. Easy to grow from seed or transplant. Resists bolting. Grows well in cool and warm temps. Harvest throughout season. Best flavor after light frost.
A/E	Lettuce	Lactuca sativa	Loose-leaf varieties for continuous cutting	Rosette	Medium to coarse	Mass, border, part shade, container	6"	6"	Great for early and late cool seasons. Wide range of leaf colors, textures. Easy to grow from seed. Fun to design with different colors. Will tolerate light shade, especially in mid-summer.

VEGETABLES *(continued)*

Code	Plant	Botanical Name	Varieties of Note	Form	Texture	Landscape Uses	Width	Height	Notes
A/E	Mustard	*Brassica juncea*	Osaka Purple, Mizuna	Rosette	Coarse	Mass, border, part shade	8–12"	12–24"	Wide range of leaf colors and textures. Minor flea beetle damage when young. Easy to grow from seed. Harvest throughout season.
A/E	Okra	*Abelmoschus esculentus*	Burgundy, Red Velvet	Upright	Medium	Specimen, height, color	18–30"	3–5'	Start seeds indoors in early spring to ensure a crop in late summer. Put this in your sunniest spot. Loves heat.
A/E	Onion	*Allium cepa*		Upright	Coarse	Mass, border, verticality	4"	12"	Wide variety of green, bunching, storage onions. Green and bunching easy to grow from seed.
A/E	Pak choi	*Brassica rapa*	Tatsoi, Purple Pak Choi	Rosette	Coarse	Border, container, part shade	6"	6"	Attractive shiny, spoon-shaped leaves on tight rosette. Dwarf varieties available. Tolerate light shade. Purple varieties particularly interesting.
A/E	Pepper	*Capsicum annuum*	Miniature Chocolate Bell, Alma Paprika, Sweet Banana, Mariachi and hundreds more!	Upright	Medium	Specimen, texture, color	18"	16–24"	Wide variety of fruit colors. Many varieties self-supporting. Easy to grow in containers.
A/E	Rhubarb	*Rheum* sp.		Upright rosette	Coarse	Mass planting, texture, color, early season interest	18–48"	18–36"	Ubiquitous in most cool-climate gardens. Hardy perennial and one of the first plants to appear in spring. Place interesting plants around it to visually take its place when done producing for the season.
A/E	Snap pea	*Pisum sativum*		Climbing	Medium	Trellis	3"	5–7'	Plant near decorative support or trellis. Plant with flowering vine (ex. Thunbergia, morning glory) for visual interest. Grows best in cool temps.
A/E	Spinach, Malabar	*Basella alba*	Red Malabar	Climbing	Medium	Trellis	12–18"	to 10 '	Striking climbing plant. Shiny foliage. Red-stemmed varieties are particularly attractive. Plant near a sturdy trellis.
A/E	Tomatillo	*Physalis sppl*	Toma Verde, Purple	Upright, trailing	Medium	Trellis, specimen	36–48"	3–4'	Determinate and indeterminate varieties are available, although this is not often noted on seed packets. Both have an open, airy form. Determinates will spread more vigorously, so a trellis works well to keep them upright and controlled.
A/E	Tomato	*Lycopersicon esculentum*	Red Currant, Cherokee Purple, Black Krim, Cuore di Bue, and thousands more!	Upright, trailing	Medium to coarse	Trellis, height	20–30"	4–6'	Wide variety of fruit shapes and colors. Be sure of determinate or indeterminate. Indeterminates will climb on decorative trellis/ arbor/fence with training. Determinates usually require support. Plant Signet marigold, basil, parsley, petunia to hide bare stems.
A/E	Zucchini	*Cucurbita pepo*	Cocozelle/Cocozella di Napoli, Italian Ribbed	Spreading	Coarse	Large space, container, texture	36–48"	12"	Choose bush varieties resistant to powdery mildew. Can be grown successfully in large container. Flowers edible.

Codes: A =Herbaceous Annual; P= Herbaceous Perennial; W=Woody; E=Edible; NE=Non-Edible

FRUITS

Code	Plant	Botanical Name	Varieties of Note	Form	Texture	Landscape Uses	Width	Height	Hardiness Zones	Notes
W/E	Apple	*Malus domesica*	Chestnut crab, Cortland, Fireside, Haralson, Honeycrisp, Honeygold, Keepsake, Sweet 16, SnowSweet, Regent, Wealthy, Zestar!	Round, open	Medium	Specimen, shade tree	8–15'	8–20'	3–9	Trees on dwarf rootstock good size for home garden. Requires annual pruning, thinning.
W/E	Apricot	*Prunus armeniaca*	Moonglow, Sunglow, Harcot, Wescot	Round, spreading	Fine to medium	Specimen, shade tree	to 20'	to 20'	4–8	Profuse, fragrant flowers in early spring. Spring frost may kill flowers. Most cold hardy varieties require another variety for pollination. Short lived (10 years).
W/E	Blueberry	*Vaccinium spp.*	Northblue, Northcountry, Northsky, St. Cloud, Polaris, Chippewa, Superior	Round	Medium	Specimen, hedge, container	3–4'	to 5'	3–10	Attractive form, leaf, fruit, fall color. Few pest/disease problems. Requires acidic soil. Good for containers. Requires at least two varieties for pollination.
W/E	Citrus, Dwarf	*Citrus spp.*	Meyer Lemon, Kaffir Lime, Key Lime	Round, open	Medium	Specimen, container	to 8'	to 10'	9–10	Great choice to grow in containers in cold climates. Bring indoors before frost. Keep in bright, warm spot until nights are above 55 degrees F. Trees can grow to 8–10', but can be kept smaller with pruning.
P/E	Cranberry	*Vaccinium macrocarpon*	Stevens	Spreading	Fine to medium	Ground cover, container	12"	6–8"	3–7	Prefer acidic, sandy soil. Best to start from cuttings or rooted plants. Spread by runners, up to 2' per year. Flowers/fruit borne on 6" upright stems after year three. Self-fertile. Limited varieties are available to the home grower.
W/E	Currant, Red	*Ribes rubrum*	Red Lake, Pink Champagne	Round	Medium to coarse	Specimen, hedge	3'	to 5'	3–8	Attractive form, leaf, fruit. Requires annual pruning. Self-fertile. Bright red, pink, white berries.
W/E	Gooseberry	*Ribes uva-crispa*	Pixwell, Hinomakke Red	Vase, irregular	Medium to coarse	Specimen, hedge, screen	3'	to 5'	3–8	Attractive leaf and fruit. Most cultivars have spines. Requires annual pruning. Self-fertile.

FRUITS *(continued)*

Code	Plant	Botanical Name	Varieties of Note	Form	Texture	Landscape Uses	Width	Height	Hardiness Zones	Notes
W/E	Grape	*Vitis spp.*	Bluebell, Swenson Red, Edelweiss, Frontenac, Fr. Gris, LaCrescent, Marquette, Marechal Foch, Seyval Blanc, St. Croix, St. Pepin	Vine	Coarse	Arbor, trellis, fence	6–8'	10–15'/ year	3–9	Requires training, annual pruning. Can tolerate drought once established. Full sun and high temps to ripen fruit. Buy plants with well-developed roots.
W/E	Kiwi, Hardy	*Actinidia kolomikta, A. arguta, A. polygama*	Arctic Beauty, Aromatnaya, Krupnopladnaya, Sentayabraskaya	Vine	Coarse	Arbor, trellis, fence	8–10'	10–15'/ year	3–9	Requires sturdy support, well-drained soil, part shade, protected site. Need male and female plants to produce fruit.
W/E	Pear	*Pyrus spp.*	Summercrisp, Ure, Gourmet, Luscious, Patten	Conical	Medium	Specimen	12–25'	to 20'	4–8	Trees can grow quite large, making some fruit difficult to harvest. Generally disease free. Requires two varieties for pollination.
W/E	Plum	*Prunus spp.*	Alderman, Mt. Royal, LaCrescent, Pipestone, Redglow, South Dakota, Superior, Underwood, Black Ice, Stanley	Round, spreading	Medium	Specimen	20'	to 20'	4–8	Profuse, fragrant flowers in early spring. Spring frost may kill flowers. Requires two varieties for pollination. Toka a good pollenizer for most varieties. Short-lived (10 years).
W/E	Pomegranate	*Punica granatum*	Wonderful, Eversweet, Granada	Round, spreading	Medium	Specimen, container	to 20'	to 20'	7–10	Generally grown as a multi-stemmed shrub, though can be trained as a tree. Tends to sucker. Container-grown shrubs in cooler regions should be brought indoors to a sunny location before fall frost. Not recommended for very cold regions.
P/E	Raspberry	*Rubus ideaus*	Caroline, Heritage, Joan J	Upright, arching	Coarse	Hedge, screen	18"	to 8'	3–8	Summer-bearing and fall-bearing cultivars available. Spread vigorously through rhizomes. Annual pruning required.
P/E	Strawberry	*Fragaria x ananassa*	Allstar, Annapolis, Cavendish, Earliglow, Honeoye, Jewel	Rosette, spreading	Medium to coarse	Ground cover, container	12"	12"	3–9	Most spread via above-ground runners. Some cultivars spread less. Attractive foliage, flowers, fruit.
P/E	Strawberry, Alpine	*Fragaria vesca*		Rosette	Medium to coarse	Ground cover, border, container	12"	12"	3–9	Smaller-fruited than common strawberry. Tolerates part shade. Non-running. Nice groundcover.

Codes: A = Herbaceous Annual; P= Herbaceous Perennial; W=Woody; E=Edible; NE=Non-Edible

HERBS

Code	Plant	Botanical Name	Varieties of Note	Form	Texture	Landscape Uses	Width	Height	Notes
A/E	Basil	Ocimum basilicum	Spicy Globe, Purple Ruffles, Dark Opal	Upright	Medium to coarse	Container, mass	8–12"	14–20"	Wide range of colors, flavors. Purple varieties add visual interest. Good companion to tomatoes, peppers, eggplant.
A/E	Chervil	Anthiscus cerefolium		Mound	Fine	Border, container	8–12"	12–18"	Light anise/parsley flavor. Very fine texture. Great for borders.
P/E	Chive	Allium schoenoprasum		Upright	Fine to medium	Beneficials, border, mass	10–12"	8–12"	Flowers edible. Attract beneficials. Spreading and self-seeding. Plant near tomatoes and apples for possible pest-control benefits.
P/E	Chive, garlic	Allium tuberosum		Upright	Fine to medium	Beneficials	10–12"	12–14"	Self-seeding. White flowers attract beneficials.
A/E	Cilantro	Coriandrum sativum		Mound	Medium	Border, container	8–12"	24–36"	Flowers edible. Attract beneficials. Spreading and self-seeding. Plant near tomatoes and apples for possible pest-control benefits.
A/E	Dill	Anethum graveolens	Bouquet	Upright	Fine	Beneficials, mass, cut flowers	8–10"	30–36"	Use for height, fragrance, fine texture. Attracts beneficials. Self-seeding. Copper color in late summer.
A/E	Fennel	Foeniculum vulgare	Perfection	Upright	Fine	Mass, beneficials	8–12"	18–24"	Use for height, fragrance, fine texture. Attracts beneficials. Self-seeding.
A/P/E	Lavender	Lavandula an gustifolia	Munstead, Hidcote	Mound	Fine	Border, container, beneficials, fragrance	12–18"	14–20"	Silvery foliage, attracts beneficials. Fragrant. Nice on borders, corners.
A/P/E	Marjoram	Origanim majoram		Mat-like, spreading	Medium	Border, container	6–8"	8–24"	Similar to oregano and thyme. Small, oval gray-green leaves. Fine spreading stems. Spills over edges of containers.
P/E	Mint	Mentha sp.		Spreading	Medium	Container, ground cover, mass	12–18"	12–36"	Vigorous and aggressive perennial. Good for containers. Many flavor and color varieties.
A/P/E	Oregano	Origanum vulgare	Greek	Mat-like	Medium	Border, ground cover, container	12"	12"	Can be perennial with good snow cover or mulch. Silvery-green foliage. Good for borders, bed corners, path edges (tolerates occasional stepping).
A/E	Parsley	Petroselinum crispum		Mound	Fine	Border, mass, container	8–12"	12–18"	Great around tomatoes, filler around root veg. Nice combined with violas. Curly and flat varieties. Harvest outer stems, leaves throughout season.
A/P/E	Rosemary	Rosmarinus officinalis		Upright or trailing	Fine	Container, ground cover	18–24"	18–36"	Good for containers, especially trailing varieties. Generally hardy in Zone 6, but may be overwintered in colder regions by mulching, bringing indoors.
P/E	Sage	Salvia officinalis	Tricolor, Golden	Mound	Medium	Border, container, mass	12–18"	12–24"	Easy to grow. Common garden sage has best flavor and is the hardiest (to Zone 3).
A/E	Savory, summer	Satureja hortensis		Upright	Fine	Border, container, mass	8–12"	12–18"	Attracts beneficials. Grows quickly from seed. Self-seeding.
P/E	Thyme	Thymus sp.		Mat-like, spreading	Fine	Ground cover, border, container	12"	12"	Mounding and trailing varieties. Good for borders, containers. Nice combined with alyssum or other small-flowered annual. Starts easily from seed.

EDIBLE FLOWERS

Code	Plant	Botanical Name	Varieties of Note	Form	Texture	Landscape Uses	Width	Height	Notes
A/E	Bachelor button	*Centaurea cyanus*		Upright	Fine to medium	Beneficials, cut flower	6"	24–36"	Petals edible. Attracts beneficials.
A/E	Borage	*Borago officinalis*		Upright	Medium to coarse	Beneficials	12"	18–24"	Petals and foliage edible. Foliage undesirable due to fuzzy texture. Petals used in salads, garnish. Attracts bees.
A/E	Calendula/ Pot marigold	*Calendula officinalis*		Upright, clump	Medium	Beneficials	8"	18–24"	Petals edible, used in salads. Adds golden color to rice, sauces. Self-seeding. Requires deadheading.
P/E	Echinacea	*Echinacea purpurea*		Upright	Medium to coarse	Beneficials, cut flower	12"	48"	Plant parts not recommended for fresh eating, but used in teas, medicinal applications. Attracts beneficials. Great for height. Native to many regions.
P/E	Monarda/ Bee balm	*Monarda sp.*		Upright	Medium	Beneficials, cut flower, naturalizing	12"	36"	M. didyma and M. fistulosa used in teas, medicinal applications. Attracts beneficials. M. fistulosa native to many regions.
A/E	Nasturtium	*Tropaeolum sp.*	Vesuvius, Alaska Mix	Mound, trailing, climbing	Medium	Mass, border	8–12"	12" to trailing	Petals, foliage, and seed pods edible. Some varieties trailing. Mainstay in edible landscape.
A/E	Signet marigold	*Tagetes tenuifolia*	Gem series	Mound	Fine	Beneficials, mass, border	12"	8"	Petals edible. Plant around base of tomatoes to hide bare stems. Mounded foliage covered with 3/4" flowers.
A/E	Sunflower	*Helianthus annuus*		Upright	Medium to coarse	Cut flower	18"	48" or more	Petals, seeds edible. Great for height. Wide variety of colors, heights.
A/E	Viola	*Viola sp.*		Mound	Fine to medium	Beneficials, mass, border	9–12"	5"	Petals edible. Borders, edges, containers. Nice paired with parsley, other herbs.

Codes: A =Herbaceous Annual; P= Herbaceous Perennial; W=Woody; E=Edible; NE=Non-Edible

ORNAMENTALS

Code	Plant	Botanical Name	Varieties of Note	Form	Texture	Landscape Uses	Width	Height	Notes
P/NE	Agastache/ Hyssop/ Licorice mint/ Hummingbird mint	Agastache sp.	Frangrant Giant Hyssop, Anise Hyssop, A. rupestris, A. neomexicana	Upright	Medium	Beneficials, background, cut flower, color, winter interest, some native	18–42"	18–36"	Species and varieties range from discreet spikes of pale purple flowers to showy reds and oranges. All are fragrant and attract many pollinators. Be sure to choose variety hardy to your zone.
A/NE	Alyssum	Lobularia maritima		Mound, creeping, clump	Fine	Beneficials, ground cover, color	6"	3–4"	Attracts beneficials. Fragrant. Combines nicely with thyme, marjoram, other small-leaved trailing herbs.
P/NE	Aster	Aster sp.	New England, Smooth, Sky Blue	Upright, mound	Fine	Beneficials, cut flower, color, winter interest, some native	12–18"	18–24"	Attracts beneficials. Many varieties native. Fluffy seed heads add interest to winter garden.
P/NE	Black-eyed susan	Rudbeckia sp.		Upright	Medium	Beneficials, color, winter interest, some native	18–24"	18–36"	Classic perennial flower. Many cultivated varieties.
A/NE	Cosmos	Cosmos bipinnatus		Upright	Fine	Beneficials, cut flower, color	12–18"	48"	Attracts beneficials. Adds lots of color. Great for height. Wide variety of colors, sizes.
P/NE	Culver's root	Veronicastrum virginicum		Upright	Medium	Native in many areas, beneficials	12–18"	48–72"	Native to many regions. Spikes of white flowers. Great for height at rear of bed. Does well in part shade.
A/P/NE	Dianthus	Dianthus sp.		Mound	Fine	Color, borders, cut flower.	6–12"	6–30"	Annual and perennial species available. Great filler for beds. Adds a lot of color.
P/NE	Goldenrod	Salidago sp.		Upright	Fine to medium	Beneficials, color, background, some native	18–24"	24–60"	Native to many regions. Fine tufts of yellow flowers atop tall plants. Great for planting at the back of the garden.
A/NE	Million bells	Calibrachoa x hybrida		Mound, trailing	Medium	Borders, containers, color	12–14"	5–10"	Great filler for borders and containers. Small, petunia-like flowers do not need deadheading. Lots of color all season. Good understory plant.
A/NE	Petunia	Petunia sp.		Mound, trailing	Medium	Ground cover, border, container, color	8–12"	8–12"	Fills in around root vegetables. Good understory plant for tomatoes.
P/NE	Prairie coneflower	Ratibidia columnifera		Upright	Medium to coarse	Beneficials, cut flower, color, some native	12–24"	24"	Attracts beneficials. Long bloom period. Native to many regions.
P/NE	Russian sage	Perovskia sp.		Upright	Fine	Beneficials, difficult soil, background, cut flower, color, winter interest	18–36"	18–48"	Great for planting at the back of beds. Very hardy, easy to grow. Attracts beneficials. Pale purple spikes of tiny flowers. Wide range of heights.
A/NE	Scarlet tasselflower	Emilia coccinea	Scarlet Magic	Upright	Fine to medium	Beneficials, color, cut flower	12"	24"	Attracts beneficials. Half-inch pincushion flowers on top of tall, thin stems. Attractive planted with kale, chard.
A/NE	Thunbergia	Thunbergia alata		Climbing, trailing	Medium	Trellis, color	15"	36"	Good complement to climbers like beans and peas. Adds color to trellises.
P/NE	Yarrow	Achillea millefolia		Upright, mound	Fine to medium	Beneficials, cut flower, color, mass planting, winter interest, some native	8–12"	8–12"	Attracts beneficials, long bloom period. Easy to grow and divide. Wide variety of colors from pale yellow to deep burgundy.
A/NE	Zinnia	Zinnia sp.		Upright	Medium to coarse	Beneficials, cut flower, color	9–12"	24–36"	Color is great contrast to coarse greens (kale, etc.). Attracts beneficials.

Codes: A =Herbaceous Annual; P= Herbaceous Perennial; W=Woody; E=Edible; NE=Non-Edible

resources

There are so many gardening websites and resources online that it can become a bit overwhelming. I've tried to find reliable resources on many of the topics covered in this book to help you sift through the wealth of information that's available. If you're searching online for information that I have not included here, it's important to know the source of that information. A good rule of thumb is to look for resources from universities (generally university extension services). These sources offer unbiased, research- and science-based information that can be trusted. This is not to say that other websites can't offer valuable content, but you can be pretty sure that universities go the extra step to make sure their content is valid. When searching for gardening advice online, I always include the word *university* in my search, which will help university-based websites come up as the first results. If university and extension information is unavailable, I look to highly regarded gardening magazines and retailers before looking at little-known sites or forums.

If a link listed here appears to be broken, try going to the home page of the institution hosting the resource and do a search for the title.

Chapter 1

Rodale Institute. "Fruits and Vegetables Are Losing Their Nutrients: Choose organic fruits and vegetables for safer and more nutritious food options." www.rodale.com/nutrients-and-organic-produce

Harvard University. Center for Health and the Global Environment. "Local and Urban Agriculture." www.chge.med.harvard.edu/programs/food/nutrition.html

Sustainable Table. "Biodiversity." www.sustainabletable.org/issues/biodiversity

Chapter 2

Michigan State University Extension. "Working with Wet Areas in the Landscape." www.oakgov.com/msu/assets/docs/publications/oc0165_wet_areas.pdf

United States Department of Agriculture. Natural Resources Conservation Service. "Soil Quality Indicators: Organic Matter." www.soils.usda.gov/sqi/publications/files/sq_fou_1.pdf

Ohio State University Extension. "Understanding Soil Microbes And Nutrient Recycling." www.ohioline.osu.edu/sag-fact/pdf/0016.pdf

University of Minnesota Extension. Soil Management Series. www.extension.umn.edu/distribution/cropsystems/ DC7398.html

Oregon State University Extension Service. "Improving Garden Soils with Organic Matter." www.extension.oregonstate.edu/ catalog/pdf/ec/ec1561.pdf

North Carolina State University. Soil Science Extension. "Soil Fertility Basics."www.plantstress.com/Articles/ min_deficiency_i/soil_fertility.pdf

Chapter 3

Virginia Cooperative Extension. "Intensive Gardening Methods." www.pubs.ext.vt.edu/426/426-335/426-335.html

Oregon State University Extension Service. "Interplanting Becoming Common Again." www.extension.oregonstate.edu/ gardening/node/1090

Cornell Cooperative Extension. "Growing Vegetables, Herbs and Annual Flowers in Containers." www.gardening.cornell.edu/ factsheets/misc/containers.pdf

University of Wisconsin Extension. "Container Gardening." www.learningstore.uwex.edu/assets/pdfs/A3382.pdf

University of Illinois Extension. "Successful Container Gardens: How to Select, Plant and Maintain." www.urbanext.illinois.edu/containergardening/

Chapter 4

National Gardening Association Weed Library. www.garden.org/weedlibrary

University of California Cooperative Extension and Agricultural Experiment Station. Weed Identification Tool. www.weedid.wisc.edu/ca/weedid.php

University of New Hampshire Cooperative Extension. "Ten Easy Steps to Prevent Common Garden Diseases." www.extension. unh.edu/resources/files/Resource000498_Rep520.pdf

University of Minnesota Extension. "Starting Seeds Indoors." www.extension.umn.edu/distribution/horticulture/m1245.html

Purdue University Cooperative Extension Service. "Starting Seeds Indoors." www.hort.purdue.edu/ext/ho-14.pdf

Michigan State University Native Plants and Ecosystems Services. "Natural Enemies." www.nativeplants.msu.edu/beneficials.htm

Chapter 5

University of Minnesota Extension. "Green Manure Cover Crops for Minnesota Gardens." www.extension.umn.edu/distribution/ horticulture/M1228.html

University of Maine Cooperative Extension. "Cover Crops for Season's End." www.umaine.edu/gardening/blog/2011/07/12/ maine-home-garden-news-11/#cover

Washington State University Extension. "Backyard Composting." www.cru.cahe.wsu.edu/cepublications/eb1784e/eb1784e.pdf

University of Minnesota Extension. "Structures for Backyard Composting." www.extension.umn.edu/distribution/ horticulture/dg5553.html

Virginia Cooperative Extension. Physiology of Pruning Fruit Trees (includes links to additional pruning resources). www.pubs.ext.vt.edu/422/422-025/422-025.html

Ohio State University Extension. "Pruning Mature Apples and Pears." www.ohioline.osu.edu/hyg-fact/1000/1150.html

North Carolina State University. "Training and Pruning Fruit Trees." www.ces.ncsu.edu/depts/hort/hil/ag29.html

Chapter 6

Purdue University. List of Garden Publications. www.hort.purdue.edu/ext/garden_pubs.html#Vegetables

University of Idaho Extension. "Fruit, Vegetables and Herbs." www.extension.uidaho.edu/idahogardens/fvh/index.htm

Cornell University. Vegetable Growing Guides. www.gardening.cornell.edu/homegardening/sceneb771.html

University of Minnesota Extension. "Gardening Information: Vegetables." www.extension.umn.edu/gardeninfo/components/ info_vegetables.html

University of Illinois Extension. Vegetable Directory. www.urbanext.illinois.edu/veggies/directory.cfm

Cornell University. "Cornell Gardening Resources: Fruit." www.gardening.cornell.edu/fruit/index.html

Cornell University. Berry Diagnostic Tool. www.fruit.cornell.edu/berrytool/

Lespinasse, J., Leterme, E. *Growing Fruit Trees: Novel Concepts and Practices for Successful Care and Management.* New York: W. W. Norton and Co., 2005.

Penn State University. College of Agricultural Sciences. "Fruit Production for the Home Gardener." www.agsci.psu.edu/fphg

Penn State University. College of Agricultural Sciences. "Pennsylvania Tree Fruit Production Guide." www.agsci.psu.edu/tfpg

Reich, Lee. *The Pruning Book, 2nd Ed.* Newtown, CT: The Taunton Press, 2010.

Rieger, Mark. *Introduction to Fruit Crops.* Binghamton, NY: The Haworth Press, 2006.

University of Illinois Extension. "Fruits." www.web.extension. illinois.edu/state/hort36.html

University of Minnesota Extension. "Gardening Information: Fruit." www.extension.umn.edu/gardeninfo/components/ info_fruit.html

University of Wisconsin Extension. "Growing Apricots, Cherries, Peaches and Plums in Wisconsin." www.learningstore.uwex.edu/assets/pdfs/A3639.PDF

Westwood, M. N. *Temperate-Zone Pomology: Physiology and Culture, 3rd Ed.* Portland, OR: Timber Press, 1993.

University of Minnesota. "Growing Hops." www.sroc.cfans.umn. edu/People/Faculty/VinceFritz/Hops/index.htm

University of Missouri Extension. "Growing Herbs at Home." www.extension.missouri.edu/explorepdf/agguides/hort/ g06470.pdf

West Virginia University Extension Service. "Growing Herbs in the Home Garden." www.wvu.edu/~agexten/hortcult/herbs/ne208hrb.htm

index